The United States Army War College

The United States Army War College educates and develops leaders for service at the strategic level while advancing knowledge in the global application of Landpower.

The purpose of the United States Army War College is to produce graduates who are skilled critical thinkers and complex problem solvers. Concurrently, it is our duty to the U.S. Army to also act as a "think factory" for commanders and civilian leaders at the strategic level worldwide and routinely engage in discourse and debate concerning the role of ground forces in achieving national security objectives.

The Strategic Studies Institute publishes national security and strategic research and analysis to influence policy debate and bridge the gap between military and academia.

The Center for Strategic Leadership contributes to the education of world class senior leaders, develops expert knowledge, and provides solutions to strategic Army issues affecting the national security community.

The Peacekeeping and Stability Operations Institute provides subject matter expertise, technical review, and writing expertise to agencies that develop stability operations concepts and doctrines.

The School of Strategic Landpower develops strategic leaders by providing a strong foundation of wisdom grounded in mastery of the profession of arms, and by serving as a crucible for educating future leaders in the analysis, evaluation, and refinement of professional expertise in war, strategy, operations, national security, resource management, and responsible command.

The U.S. Army Heritage and Education Center acquires, conserves, and exhibits historical materials for use to support the U.S. Army, educate an international audience, and honor soldiers—past and present.

D0896395

STRATEGIC STUDIES INSTITUTE

The Strategic Studies Institute (SSI) is part of the U.S. Army War College and is the strategic-level study agent for issues related to national security and military strategy with emphasis on geostrategic analysis.

The mission of SSI is to use independent analysis to conduct strategic studies that develop policy recommendations on:

- Strategy, planning, and policy for joint and combined employment of military forces;

- Regional strategic appraisals;

- The nature of land warfare;

- Matters affecting the Army's future;

- The concepts, philosophy, and theory of strategy; and,

- Other issues of importance to the leadership of the Army.

Studies produced by civilian and military analysts concern topics having strategic implications for the Army, the Department of Defense, and the larger national security community.

In addition to its studies, SSI publishes special reports on topics of special or immediate interest. These include edited proceedings of conferences and topically oriented roundtables, expanded trip reports, and quick-reaction responses to senior Army leaders.

The Institute provides a valuable analytical capability within the Army to address strategic and other issues in support of Army participation in national security policy formulation.

Strategic Studies Institute
and
U.S. Army War College Press

MASTERING THE GRAY ZONE:
UNDERSTANDING A CHANGING
ERA OF CONFLICT

Michael J. Mazarr

December 2015

*****

Comments pertaining to this report are invited and should be forwarded to: Director, Strategic Studies Institute and U.S. Army War College Press, U.S. Army War College, 47 Ashburn Drive, Carlisle, PA 17013-5010.

*****

All Strategic Studies Institute (SSI) and U.S. Army War College (USAWC) Press publications may be downloaded free of charge from the SSI website. Hard copies of this report may also be obtained free of charge while supplies last by placing an order on the SSI website. SSI publications may be quoted or reprinted in part or in full with permission and appropriate credit given to the U.S. Army Strategic Studies Institute and U.S. Army War College Press, U.S. Army War College, Carlisle, PA. Contact SSI by visiting our website at the following address: *www.StrategicStudiesInstitute.army.mil.*

*****

The Strategic Studies Institute and U.S. Army War College Press publishes a monthly email newsletter to update the national security community on the research of our analysts, recent and forthcoming publications, and upcoming conferences sponsored by the Institute. Each newsletter also provides a strategic commentary by one of our research analysts. If you are interested in receiving this newsletter, please subscribe on the SSI website at *www.StrategicStudiesInstitute.army.mil/newsletter.*

ISBN 1-58487-712-X

CONTENTS

FOREWORD

This manuscript examines the increasingly important form of rivalry and statecraft that has become known as "gray zone strategies." In regions from Eastern Europe to the South China Sea, such tactics in the hands of ambitious regional powers pose a growing challenge to U.S. and allied interests. This monograph aims to provide a broad introduction to the issue to help leaders in the U.S. Army and the wider joint Department of Defense and national security community better understand this challenge. Dr. Michael Mazarr, a Senior Political Scientist at the RAND Corporation and Associate Program Director of the Army's Arroyo Center there, defines the issue, examines the most notable current cases of gray zone strategies, offers several hypotheses about the nature of this form of conflict, and suggests a number of policy responses.

The monograph emphasizes that many gray zone tools and techniques have been employed for centuries. But the analysis rightly contends that such approaches have renewed relevance, both because some new technologies have made them more effective than ever and because several major powers are making extensive use of gray zone campaigns.

We hope that the report will be of interest to audiences throughout the U.S. Army and in the wider defense community. Many U.S. commands, offices, departments, and services are grappling with the practical implications of gray zone strategies.

This research can help inform their understanding of the challenge and point the way to effective responses.

DOUGLAS C. LOVELACE, JR.
Director
Strategic Studies Institute and
    U.S. Army War College Press

ABOUT THE AUTHOR

MICHAEL J. MAZARR is a Senior Political Scientist at the RAND Corporation. Prior to coming to RAND, he spent 12 years as Professor of National Security Strategy, course director, and Associate Dean at the U.S. National War College in Washington, DC. From late-2008 to early-2010, he served as Special Assistant to the Chairman of the Joint Chiefs of Staff. From October 2000 to November 2001, he was president and chief executive officer of the Henry L. Stimson Center. Before coming to Stimson, he was senior vice president for strategic planning and development at the Electronic Industries Alliance in Arlington, VA. He has been a U.S. Naval Reserve intelligence officer, a term member of the Council on Foreign Relations, and a founding member of both the Council on Security Cooperation in Asia-Pacific and the Committee on Nuclear Policy. He taught as an adjunct professor in the Georgetown University Security Studies Program from 1989 to 2012 and again beginning in 2015. From 1993 to 1995, Dr. Mazarr was legislative assistant for foreign affairs and chief writer in the office of Representative Dave McCurdy (D-OK), where he was responsible for foreign affairs issues and legislation and the drafting of major political speeches. Before working in Congress, Mazarr was a senior fellow in international security studies at the Center for Strategic and International Studies (CSIS), Washington, DC, and oversaw major Center studies in a number of substantive areas. From 1995 to 1999, Dr. Mazarr served as editor of *The Washington Quarterly*, director of the New Millennium Project, and dean of the Young Leaders Program at CSIS. He has authored ten books, including *North Korea and the Bomb: A Case Study in Nonproliferation* (1995) and

Unmodern Men in the Modern World: Radical Islam, Terrorism, and the War on Modernity (2007). He has edited seven anthologies; published essays in *The Economist, Policy Review, Survival, The New Republic, The National Interest, Foreign Affairs, Foreign Policy, The Washington Quarterly, International Security,* and elsewhere; and authored editorials in *The Washington Post, The New York Times,* and other newspapers. Dr. Mazarr holds A.B. and M.A. degrees in government and national security studies from Georgetown University, and a Ph.D. in policy analysis from the University of Maryland School of Public Affairs.

CHAPTER 1

INTRODUCTION

In the remote reaches of the South China Sea in the Spratly Island chain, China is creating land. In order to bolster its claims to the waters of the region, Beijing is pouring millions of metric tons of sand and concrete onto submerged reefs, creating artificial islands.[1] Island-building is merely one of the most obvious of many actions, ranging from propaganda to economic coercion and swarming fleets of fishing vessels, that China has been taking to solidify its assertion of territorial and resource rights throughout the region.[2] Step by forceful step, China is laying the groundwork for a new order in the region that recognizes Beijing's unquestioned primacy, and for an international system whose norms and institutions reflect China's interests and preferences.[3] "China is biding its time," one report recently concluded, "slowly eroding American credibility in the region, changing facts on the ground where it believes it can and carefully calibrating the coercion of its rivals in the South China Sea."[4]

This series of actions is a powerful example of an approach being used by more and more states with partial, but still obvious, revisionist intent—that is to say, states dissatisfied with the status quo and determined to change important aspects of the global distribution of power and influence in their favor. Unwilling to risk major escalation with outright military adventurism, these actors are employing sequences of gradual steps to secure strategic leverage. The efforts remain below thresholds that would generate a powerful U.S. or international response, but nonetheless are forceful and deliberate, calculated to gain measurable traction over time. In one important sense, they are classic "salami-slicing" strategies, fortified with a range of emerging gray area or unconventional techniques — from cyberattacks to information campaigns to energy diplomacy. They maneuver in the ambiguous no-man's-land between peace and war, reflecting the sort of aggressive, persistent, determined campaigns characteristic of warfare but without the overt use of military force.

China's use of gradual, multi-instrument strategies to amass a decisive legal foundation for its claims in the South China Sea represents the leading example of this approach.[5] But Russia's recent actions in Eastern Europe, while employing far more direct action and violence, also constitute a variety of the tactic. Iran's pursuit of nuclear weapons and regional influence can also be viewed as a variety of gray zone strategy.[6] Even the burgeoning diplomatic and economic strategies of such rising powers as Brazil, Turkey, and India can be seen as much more restrained, but still notable, examples of gray zone campaigns.

This monograph suggests that large-scale operations in this indistinct landscape will be the dominant form of state-to-state rivalry in the coming decades. Henceforth, international rivalry may be characterized largely by such campaigns, which go today by a confusing array of names — unconventional, hybrid, gradualist, nonlinear, unrestricted, and more. This monograph aims to survey these analyses and bring analytical coherence to the issue.

To be clear, this report does not contend that gray zone approaches will be the only form of emerging conflict. As stressed, major combat — traditional warfare — remains possible, though unlikely. Hybrid warfare sits at a different place on the spectrum of conflict and is likely to be employed by various combatants. Rivals can still compete at the low end of the spectrum through classic diplomacy and covert operations. Gray zone campaigns therefore reflect only one challenge in an emerging mosaic of conflict.

Nor does this analysis contend that gray zone tactics are entirely new. States have been using these kinds of approaches for centuries, in some ways for millennia. Concepts such as political destabilization, support for proxies and militias, information campaigns, and much more have been a staple of statecraft since the city states of ancient Greece were vying for influence. This analysis contends, however, that there are at least three reasons why we should pay more attention to gray zone issues. First, a number of leading aggressive powers—notably China, Russia, and Iran—appear to be making extensive use of these strategies. Second, the cost of major aggression has become so severe, and economic and social interdependence so powerful, that states with some degree of aggressive intent arguably will be in the market for alternative ways to achieve their goals. These realities increase the incentive to use gray zone approaches. Finally, while some gray zone tools have been used since ancient times, others—such as cyber weapons, advanced forms of information campaigns, and elaborate civilian tools of statecraft such as coast guards—are relatively recent and lend growing intensity to these campaigns. For all these reasons, a very old and well-established set of strategic tools has taken on increasing importance.

The concept of gray zone conflict has been increasingly evident in U.S. military writings over the last 2 years. The 2015 *National Military Strategy* characterizes the future military environment as a "continuum" on which many forms of conflict short of major war are likely to be a focus of U.S. defense policy.[7] At an April 2015 U.S. Army War College conference, Deputy Secretary of Defense Robert Work argued that adversaries were increasingly using:

> agents, paramilitaries, deception, infiltration, and persistent denial to make those avenues of approach very hard to detect, operating in what some people have called 'the gray zone.' Now, that's the zone in which our ground forces have not traditionally had to operate, but one in which they must now become more proficient.[8]

A number of U.S. Army sources, especially in the special operations community, have given increasing attention to gray zone issues.[9]

This monograph argues that three elements—rising revisionist intent, a form of strategic gradualism, and unconventional tools—are creating a new approach to the pursuit of aggressive aims, a new standard form of conflict. Evidence from a number of sources, including ongoing campaigns by China and Russia, suggests that gradual gray zone strategies may be becoming the tool of choice for states wanting to reframe the global order in the 21st century.[10] The idea of competing below the threshold of major war is hardly new: States and nonstate actors have employed gray zone approaches for thousands of years, most ambitiously during World War II and the Cold War. Nonetheless, this analysis finds reason to believe that gray zone conflict represents an identifiable and intentional strategy for several states, and a phenomenon of growing importance. If that hypothesis is valid, then the United States needs to become adept at operating in this environment.

This report represents an initial, exploratory analysis, one aimed at defining and categorizing the issue and offering an initial set of plausible conclusions about the phenomenon. It works to distinguish the concept of gray zone strategies from related notions such as hybrid, nonlinear, and unconventional warfare. It then lays out seven hypotheses about the emerging form of conflict, which together can help bound and define the challenge. The report concludes with recommendations for U.S. policies, strategies and capabilities that could help deal with this form of conflict.

One of its most important themes is that gray zone strategies carry significant potential costs and limitations. They are not magic wands or panaceas for basic strategic dilemmas. Though they attempt to remain under certain thresholds that would trigger escalatory responses, they tend to generate balancing behavior that cancels out a significant proportion of their intended results. Even gray zone aggression marks its authors as threatening and operating outside the bounds of acceptable behavior in the context of international rules, norms, and institutions. It may slide under key thresholds, but it cannot escape notice as a form of aggression. The limitations of such campaigns mean that an effective response can be mounted, and the concluding chapter of this monograph suggests an overall strategy for dealing with such tactics.

ENDNOTES - CHAPTER 1

1. See, for example, Rupert Wingfield-Hayes, "China's Island Factory," BBC Online, September 9, 2014, available from *www.bbc.co.uk/news/special/2014/newsspec_8701/index.html*. Carl Thayer has argued that commentators should not declare that China is "reclaiming land," which implies a legitimate maritime claim; it is

creating artificial island with no maritime rights significance, he argues. See Carl Thayer, "No, China is Not Reclaiming Land in the South China Sea," *The Diplomat*, June 7, 2015.

2. In June 2015, Beijing, China, announced that it would "complete" its land reclamation project "soon"; see "China to 'Complete' South China Sea Land Reclamation," BBC News, June 16, 2015.

3. There is a lively debate about the true nature of China's objectives in the region. The argument here will not portray China as an unlimited revisionist determined to conquer other states, or even one with clearly imperialist ambitions. But there seems a broad consensus that China believes it has a natural right to geopolitical primacy throughout key regions close to its borders. See, for example, Gregory Chin and Ramesh Thakur, "Will China Change the Rules of Global Order?" *The Washington Quarterly*, Vol. 33, No. 4, October 2010; Thomas J. Christensen, "Obama and Asia: Confronting the China Challenge," *Foreign Affairs*, Vol., 94, No. 5, September/October 2015; Aaron L. Friedberg, *A Contest for Supremacy: China, America, and the Struggle for Mastery in Asia*, New York: W. W. Norton, 2011; and Adam P. Liff and G. John Ikenberry, "Racing Toward Tragedy? China's Rise, Military Competition in the Asia Pacific and the Security Dilemma," *International Security*, Vol. 39, No. 2, Fall 2014.

4. Christopher Yung and Patrick McNulty, "China's Tailored Coercion and Its Rivals' Actions and Responses: What the Numbers Tell Us," Washington, DC: Center for a New American Security, January 2015, p. 13.

5. As one analyst has warned, "China's furtive, incremental encroachments into neighboring countries' borderlands . . . have emerged as a key destabilizing element in the Asian security landscape." Brahma Chellany, "China's Salami-Slice Strategy," *Japan Times*, July 25, 2013.

6. "Tehran has proven to be adept at such salami-slicing tactics," one source has concluded, gradually accumulating elements of nuclear capacity without crossing any obvious red lines that would generate a violent answer. Mark Fitzpatrick, "Report on Iran Nuclear Program: Situation Not Yet Hopeless," *al-Monitor*,

August 31, 2012. The same issue is brought up in terms of a potential Iranian breakout from an agreement, which would not be, as George Shultz and Henry Kissinger have argued, a clear-cut event. More likely it will occur, if it does, via the gradual accumulation of ambiguous evasions" which would pose serious challenges to U.S. diplomacy. See George P. Shultz and Henry Kissinger, "The Iran Deal and Its Consequences," *The Wall Street Journal*, April 7, 2015.

7. U.S. Joint Chiefs of Staff, *The National Military Strategy of the United States of America 2015* Washington, DC: Department of Defense (DoD), June 2015, pp. 3-4.

8. Deputy Secretary of Defense Robert Work, Speech at the U.S. Army War College Strategy Conference, April 8, 2015, available from *www.defense.gov/Speeches/Speech.aspx?SpeechID=1930*.

9. As just two examples, see Claudette Ruolo, "SOCOM Commander: Success Depends on Total Force Readiness," DoD News, March 26, 2015, available from *www.defense.gov/news/newsarticle. aspx?id=128461*; and Chuck Oldham, "SOCOM: Navigating the Gray Zone," Defense Media Network, June 23, 2015, available from *www.defensemedianetwork.com/stories/socom-navigating-the-gray-zone/*. The U.S. Special Operations Command released a 2014 white paper on "Counter-Unconventional Warfare"; see the coverage at Robert A. Newson, "Counter-Unconventional Warfare is the Way of the Future. How Can We Get There?" Defense in Depth Blog, Washington, DC: Council on Foreign Relations, October 23, 2014, available from *blogs.cfr.org/davidson/2014/10/23/ counter-unconventional-warfare-is-the-way-of-the-future-how-can-we-get-there/*.

10. Nonstate actors could also make profitable use of gradualist approaches, but this analysis focuses on state actors. The use of such strategies by nonstate actors could have unique features that make them best left for a separate treatment.

CHAPTER 2

MEASURED REVISIONISM:
THE ENGINE OF GRAY ZONE CAMPAIGNS

In the 2002 version of the *National Security Strategy*, the George W. Bush administration suggested that classic balance-of-power theories of state rivalry had become obsolete. Because of shared interests in areas such as trade and counterterrorism, the world's major powers now had grown to share many interests in common. More than that, the document argued that leading powers were converging on a "a single sustainable model for national success: freedom, democracy, and free enterprise." It went on:

> Today, the international community has the best chance since the rise of the nation-state in the 17th century to build a world where great powers compete in peace instead of continually prepare for war. Today, the world's great powers find ourselves on the same side — united by common dangers of terrorist violence and chaos. The United States will build on these common interests to promote global security. We are also increasingly united by common values. Russia is in the midst of a hopeful transition, reaching for its democratic future and a partner in the war on terror. Chinese leaders are discovering that economic freedom is the only source of national wealth.[1]

Developments since 2002 suggest that these claims are only half true. Major powers do share common interests, and collectively benefit from many aspects of a rules-based order. Russia profits from integrated and stable energy markets, China from global trade accords and free passage of trade. All are threatened by terrorism, piracy, global warming, and other common dangers.

Yet, these mutual interests do not imply that all major states are satisfied with the existing order. A number of rising powers are frustrated with current patterns of influence or goods, or the shape of rules and norms, and have assembled campaigns to transform that order in service of their interests and values. Such powers are neither status-quo nor militaristic; they are both integrated into the world community and deeply exasperated with it. We might call them "measured revisionists."

If world politics were composed solely of status-quo powers, there would be little engine of gray zone conflict. If it were brimming with bellicose military predators, then the primary threat would be of traditional combined arms warfare. But an analysis of the revisionist strategies of key rising powers suggests that neither of these things is true. Instead, the emerging pattern may be an ambiguous and complex middle ground—a growing number of states determined to use tools below the threshold of war to shift international rules, norms, distribution of goods, and patterns of authority to their benefit. They are the leading architects of gray zone campaigns today and likely to remain so for the foreseeable future.

This analysis is not meant to suggest that only measured revisionists, or revisionists more generally, would use gray zone strategies. The United States and other countries have employed many tools and techniques characteristic of this form of conflict, from propaganda to information operations to covert and proxy operations. But the most persistent and forceful of such strategies will issue from revisionist states, who have the most urgent motive to force change. But to be clear, to the degree that gray zone conflict becomes a more typical pattern in world politics, it will be used in ambitious and active ways by a broad range of actors.

Measured revisionism is not inherently an aggressive or adventuristic viewpoint. It is, in a sense, entirely natural to the worldview of rising powers. Such states recognize the value of a rule-based order and harbor no interest in aggressive wars. But they are ambitious; they do demand and presume a transformation of some elements of the system; and they therefore possess a motive to seek out deliberate but powerful strategies for change.

RECOGNIZING REVISIONISTS

A number of revisionist or dissatisfied powers appear to be in the market for options to transform the status quo. They are frustrated with various aspects of their current position—their degree of regional or global influence, their ability to shape international rules and institutions to their benefit, the looming authority of U.S. power—and want to engineer a future international order more of their own design. Such a mindset can be found not only in China, Russia, and Iran, but also, in different ways, nations like Brazil, Turkey, and India.

Scholars and analysts seldom define what they mean by a revisionist or dissatisfied state, and developing criteria to usefully distinguish status quo from revisionist actors can be exceptionally difficult.[2] Recent U.S. actions, for example, in Afghanistan, Iraq, Libya, and Syria, and in self-consciously advocating for democratic revolutions from North Africa to eastern Europe, would meet many of the conditions commonly associated with revisionism. The United States has rejected or failed to ratify a long list of international accords. In order to pose revisionists against an "international order," moreover, that order must be understood in specific enough terms to know when a state was trying to undermine it. Just how many elements of the rule-based order a country would need to oppose to be counted as a revisionist is unclear.

Existing definitions generally point to states that have some burning reason for overturning major elements of the existing system.[3] One scholar defines revisionists as "states not satisfied with the status quo and interested in pursuing goals more expansive than strict defensive-minded security maximization." More specifically, revisionism demands "a preference for changing the international distribution of goods — including, but not limited to, territory — and a willingness to incur costs in pursuing that preference."[4] Another analyst suggests that "Revisionist states seek to change the distribution of goods (for example, territory) among the great powers in international relations, while status-quo states prefer to keep things as they are."[5] In one of the leading recent assessments of the issue, Randall Schweller argued that "staying in place is not the primary goal of revisionist states. They want to increase, not just preserve, their core values and to improve their position in the system." As a result, they "must gain relative to others."[6]

Beyond this general desire for transformation of existing power relations, revisionists have often been viewed as willing to undertake **military** adventurism.[7] The focus on military aggression characterizes the related concept of rogue states, which was discussed widely as a leading challenge for U.S. foreign policy in the 1990s. Rogue states, explains one analysis, are states that "have been effectively labeled as persistent and/or grave violators of core norms of the international community."[8] Perhaps the most common definition of rogues involves a combination of support for terrorism and pursuit of weapons of mass destruction, usually combined with repression at home.[9] Secretary of State Madeleine Albright gave a 1998 speech in which she referred to rogues as "those that not only do not have a part in the international system, but whose very being involved being outside of it and throwing, literally, hand grenades inside in order to destroy it."[10]

These characteristics, however, go beyond what I have in mind with the concept of a measured revisionist. This category of states has powerful interests wrapped up in sustaining most elements of the international system, and much of their behavior fits easily into the category of "responsible stakeholders" in that system. They also crave the recognition that comes from such inclusion—most fear and resent being labeled as the sort of marginal troublemakers implied by the rogue state category. These characteristics are critical to understanding the emerging pattern of conflict, because it is precisely in the limited, mixed, and sometimes paradoxical motives of measured revisionists that we find the basis for gradual, constrained forms of nonmilitary conflict.

A CHALLENGING CONCEPT

Categories can be as misleading as they are helpful, masking differences between individual states in the effort to shape them into meaningful groups. In the context of understanding gray zone conflict, the notion of measured revisionism can be helpful in describing the origins and engines of such strategies. But it is important to recognize some of the potential analytical challenges with this category.

To begin, the very idea of a revisionist state is likely to embody some degree of imprecision. Dozens of states seek to "change" the international system in some way, and it is not clear what precisely a state needs to do in order to be labeled a "revisionist power." The significance of their motivations and intentions lies precisely in how **much** they seek to change the system, and in what way, but these nuances can be lost in a generic framework.

It is also difficult to recognize states intent on changing the international order without a clear definition of that order. George Modelski has offered a set of potential factors, indicating that states are concerned with several specific aspects of order: Security, bargaining power, market access, and ability to shape the rules of the system.[11] Designating states as rogues or renegades presumes some agreed order whose rules they are violating.[12] Some of the ambiguity of such definitions arises when trying to identify states interested in transforming the international system: Just how many specific issues must they attempt to revise before they count as "revisionists"?

For the purposes of this analysis, I consider states revisionist if they aim to substantially transform, to their benefit, significant international rules or norms, the structure or operating procedures of international organizations, the balance of power or influence among states, or the distribution of international goods. Revisionists view existing global rules, institutions, norms, and power balances as insufficient to meet their goals, or unjust, or biased against them, or some combination of all of these.

Even defined this way, however, it can be difficult to distinguish revisionism from classic great power competition. In the realist portrait of world politics, states are always jockeying to enhance their relative power—meaning that they are all dissatisfied with their present standing to some degree. They aim to change the distribution of goods and influence in their favor. From the standpoint of the broader model being developed here of gray zone rivalry, all great powers are constantly using a wide range of instruments to enhance their position. Yet, in discussing the category of rogue or "renegade" states, Miroslav Nincic suggests that the threat they pose has partly "supplanted classical power politics as the distinctive feature of international politics."[13] We will need clear criteria, then, to distinguish a true revisionist from a run-of-the-mill, self-interested great power—and to distinguish day-to-day great power competition from what could be understood as more elaborate, formalized gray zone conflict.

The idea that rising states typically pick up more revisionist goals as they become more powerful is also too simple. As states rise, they gain power to revise the order, but also, usually, growing interests in stability and predictability. As states become more powerful and developed, they also tend to become more conservative—they have a greater stake in the system, and tend to develop domestic interest groups whose power and prosperity depends on a functioning international order. It is no accident, then, that many mature states tend to be status-quo states: Once they have certain capabilities and power, they simply do not need to revise the system as much. (We can see this trend, for example, in China's approach to nonproliferation. For decades, Beijing was resistant to any controls that would undercut its ability to develop a deterrent. Once a reliable deterrent was in place, it embraced a range of international accords.)

Nor do many discussions speak to the reasons **why** states become revisionist. There can be many such reasons: Pressure from domestic interest groups; the ambitions and personality of specific leaders; or state capacity — the idea that states will attempt to revise the system to their benefit when they believe they have sufficient power to do so. The reasons why states seek revisionist goals can be all-important in understanding the degree of threat or challenge they pose to U.S. interests and the international order.

Ideas and ideology play a particularly significant role in driving the preferences of revisionist states. Ideological motivations provide one important indicator in distinguishing revisionists from run-of-the-mill great powers. While great powers are interested in greater power for generic reasons, true revisionists tend to act in service of a nationalist vision grounded in grand narratives. Revisionists are often frustrated states who believe the international system is biased against them and possess passionately-held ideas of their rightful place in the world. Their desire to change the system comes not merely from a bloodless calculation of relative gains, but from an emotional sense, grounded in historical myths, that they have been called by destiny to play a greater role in the world.

DEGREES OF REVISIONISM

It is critical, therefore, to realize that there are different varieties of revisionists, and that the boundaries between revisionism and other typologies of states are indistinct. There are the extreme cases, David Zionts has explained, like Nazi Germany, which "fail to moderate even when survival is at stake." Much more common, though — and he gives the example of Iran during the period of the Iran-Iraq war—are cases of states which, "while ultimately aiming to avoid self-destruction will nonetheless persist in revisionist aims in spite of compelling external factors." The difference, in other words, is between "those that respond to failure or other systemic changes by moderating their revisionism and those that persist." Zionts refers to the two categories as "reasonable" and "unreasonable" revisionists.[14]

Randall Schweller distinguishes four types of states on the status quo-revisionist spectrum. He describes "lions," states ready to fight for what they have but indifferent about taking risk to gain more; "lambs," countries hesitant even to defend what they have; "jackals," anxious to gain power but obsessed with preserving what they have and thus risk-averse even as they are opportunistic; and "wolves," belligerent predators determined to gain more and willing to undertake massive risk, "even if losing the gamble means extinction." Relaxed about "the fear of loss, [wolves] are free to pursue reckless expansion."[15]

These analogies are only suggestive, but they provide a framework for thinking about the challenge posed by various states today. By Schweller's standards, there have been very few true wolves. He provides Hitler's Germany as an example, and Saddam's Iraq may be a modern counterpart, though, even in that case, Saddam was risk averse in important ways. A key question for the future is the status of the chief antagonists to the current system—China, Russia, and Iran. None of them are close to being a wolf; all are too risk-averse. But they seem more determinedly revisionist than Schweller's "jackals," which are largely opportunistic rather than calculating.

There might be room for at least one additional category of state: States partially satisfied with the existing system but determined to gain a larger share of influence within it. These states will be more persistent and calculating in promoting their agenda than the more opportunistic jackals, but will not rank anywhere close to wolves in their suicidal urge to power. They will not merely be on the lookout for opportunities; they will follow long-term campaigns designed to enhance their influence relative to others, and especially to the leading states in the system. But they will not want to push these efforts to the point of jeopardizing the entire system, from which they enjoy regime-sustaining benefits. These would be the measured revisionists.

Another way of categorizing revisionists is to look for specific criteria that can be used to locate them on a spectrum of state behavior. Alastair Iain Johnston has offered five such criteria to measure revisionist intent on the part of a state actor.[16] They are:

1. Low participation rates in regulatory international institutions.

2. Participation in the institutions without actually accepting norms.

3. Participation and norm-following, but opportunistic, ventures to change the rules of the game "in ways that defeat the original purposes of the institution and the community."

4. An internalized preference for "a radical redistribution of material power in the international system."

5. Actions to achieve such a redistribution, especially by military force.

We might add other indicators to Johnston's helpful list. These could include strength of revisionist ideology: Is the state or regime built on a narrative that speaks to a requirement to overturn elements of the system? Another factor could be resoluteness: Is the state fully committed to revisionism or is its interest in changing balances of power episodic and variable? The role of military force offers another criterion: To what degree is the state prepared to use military aggression to achieve a redistribution of power? True revisionists perceive military power as the leading tool to overturn existing orders and reorient power relationships.

Figure 2-1 outlines out a typology of regime types relative to status quo or revisionist orientation. Posing the types as a spectrum simplifies a more complex relationship of variables, but the typology does convey some of the basic distinctions involved. For the purposes of this analysis, the category of most interest is that of measured revisionism — states that do not meet the classic predatory characteristics of militaristic revisionists, but are nonetheless determined to change the system in comprehensive ways, beyond the issue-specific desire for reform of what I call "targeted revisionists."

Passive Status Quo ("Lambs")	Active Status Quo ("Lions")	Targeted Revisionist	Measured Revisionist	Opportunistic Predator ("Jackals")	Reckless Predator ("Wolves")
No motive to overturn system or gain relative advantage; limited investment in current-patterns. Security through appeasement and bandwagoning.	Powerful defense of existing status, supports rules-based order, little motive for aggressive relative gains acquisition. Self-defense, balancing.	Satisfied power with no motive to harm system, but revisionist and risk-accepting on a few issues; little ethno-nationalist motivation; sensitive to relative power, violent in defense of order.	Primary goal is preserving power; favors many elements of global order, but dissatisfied with current status, power relations and rule sets; strong nationalist narratives and motivation; determined to enhance relative power.	Seeks change in power balance, but risk-averse and self-protective; values security of regime more than change in status; will ally with lions as well as wolves.	Values relative gains more than security. Highly risk-tolerant and aggressive. Doctrinal or ideological requirement to spread territory. Determined to upset system. Unlimited aims.
Sweden	United Kingdom	United States	China	North Korea	Nazi Germany

Source: Four of the categories and their characteristics are drawn from Randall Schweller, "Bandwagoning for Profit: Bringing the Revisionist State Back In," *International Security*, Vol. 19, No. 1, Summer 1994, pp. 100-104.

Figure 2-1. Typologies of State Preference: Status Quo Versus Revisionist.

By this standard, China, Russia, and Iran would seem to count as measured revisionists—but so are a dozen other rising powers determined to capture more influence. Their interests are not absolute or even always very clear, which increases their appetite for more cautious and gradual approaches as opposed to risky and urgent ones. Meantime these revisionists are not uncompromising; they do not seek to bring down the existing international order, many aspects of which clearly serve their interests, so much as they hope to remold, shape, and modify it to enhance their own standing. Their interests and objectives in these revisionist campaigns are thus limited.

Within this typology, perhaps the most important distinctions lie in the middle of the spectrum. Status quo powers are of little concern, and there are few real jackals or wolves—and when they exist, they generally spark balancing behavior that mitigates their threat. Moreover, while such states may use gray zone strategies, it will be in service of larger aggressive aims that spread into traditional military aggression. Figure 2-2 offers a framework for comparing the more common types of states.[17]

	Active Status Quo	Targeted Revisionists	Measured Revisionists
Basic objective	Preserve stability and status quo distribution of power; reinforce norms and institutions	Generally preserve status quo but also change a small number of specific aspects of power / goods distribution	Support many aspects of rules-based order but transform international order in key aspects of power dynamics and rule-setting influence
Example state / actions	Germany / support for global economic norms	United States / defense of global order but also quasi-revisionist support for democratic revolutions	China / sponsorship of alternative economic and regional strategic institutions
Role in global institutions	Strong, supportive, respect norms and rules	Strong though willing to strike out unilaterally when pushing on targeted issue of revisionist intent	Mixed: Strong and supportive role on majority of rules/norms that benefit interests; active effort to subvert norms and institutions in revisionist areas

Figure 2-2. Comparing Moderate Revisionisms.

	Active Status Quo	Targeted Revisionists	Measured Revisionists
Risk tolerance	Limited for actions that revise elements of system; stronger but still constrained for actions deemed necessary to respond to challenges	Higher in areas identified as needing change; limited tolerance for risk in areas of military adventurism or outright conflict; higher tolerance for diplomatic, economic initiatives	Higher across the board but especially in non-military areas where dangers of outright conflict can seemingly be controlled
Identity-based motivations	Largely satisfied with identity and role in overall system	Largely satisfied but having usually rationalistic belief in, or sometimes moral commitment to, value or advantages of changing specified elements of system	Significant degree of frustration about relative identity, role and degree of recognition in international system. Impulse for change comes in part from grievance over insufficient identity. Strongly-felt ethno-nationalist commitment to regional hegemony and global influence

Figure 2-2. Comparing Moderate Revisionisms. (cont.)

MEASURED REVISIONISTS AND INTERNATIONAL POLITICS

Measured revisionists therefore represent a strange hybrid, a largely cautious, conservative state determined to foster a transformation of the international order. They are determined to revise power relationships but aim to do so without causing general mayhem. They are risk-averse, to a degree, except with regard to a tiny handful of core vital interests that would provoke violence. The majority of their actions may fall squarely into the basket of responsible stakeholders in the global system. As world politics grow more multipolar and more characterized by regional and global rivalries, more states seem to be joining this ambiguous category.

An especially important characteristic of such re-visionists relates to the sources of their motivations. Despite the lack of an ideological requirement for expansion per se, these are frustrated powers, believing that they ought to have a more dominant role in world politics than they do. The range of measured revisionists proposed here is fairly broad, and they will have a very wide array of types and degrees of frustrations — Brazil's sense of grievance, as an example, is nothing like Russia's. Nonetheless, in all cases, the national narratives of these states speak to a glorious destiny in the community of nations, and they feel that others have not offered sufficient degrees of recognition or respect. This identity-fueled grievance gives some of these powers a wary worldview and makes them less likely to trust in norms, rules, or institutions built primarily by others.

Nonetheless, even the more aggressive members of this group are likely to end up as measured revisionists rather than wolves or even jackals. They gain substantial benefits from the rules-based international order. They participate in its capital markets, rely on foreign direct investment and international loans, sell or buy in global energy markets, ship goods that require stability of sea lanes, produce technologies that demand reliable standard-setting, and more.

But there is a more subtle way in which many states, even with revisionist intent, rely on the international system: For recognition, another fuel of legitimacy. They crave leadership **among** the global society of states, even if they believe that some of the leaders of the current order (specifically the United States) are hostile to their power and goals. These are not states, at least in their current guise, prepared to act in violent contravention of all major global norms.

These are not Hitler's Germany, or Saddam's Iraq, or Kim Il-sung's North Korea. They aspire to middle-class prosperity and global leadership in a modern, cosmopolitan guise; their identity narratives demand respect for their place in the world community, not the subjugation of others.

Measured revisionists, therefore, will strongly support elements of that order, actively participating and investing in key institutions, voting at the United Nations to enforce key norms, working actively to enforce important rules. They will join diplomatic or even military coalitions, especially for generally-supported norm-building activities like humanitarian endeavors or combatting organized crime, piracy or terrorism. They will crave membership in international fora, host important standard-setting bodies and Track 2 processes. The complexity of their motives and behavior derives from the fact that, despite the interests they express with such norm- and institution-reinforcing actions, they remain committed to achieving specific ends that demand a significant change in existing power structures and rule-setting influence.

I would define these prudent, circumspect measured revisionists as having the following basic characteristics.

1. They benefit substantially, in some cases decisively, from engagement with the international community, and have little interest in destabilizing world politics.

2. They gain advantage from participation in international institutions and diplomatic initiatives, and want to preserve the ability to cooperate with other leading states when their interests call for collective problem-solving.

3. They are nonetheless dissatisfied with the current global balance of power and the U.S./Western degree of dominance in articulating and enforcing global norms.

4. They possess historical, cultural, and political motives to see themselves as natural leaders, in regional as well as global terms, and believe themselves destined and entitled to a certain amount of hegemony over neighbors.

5. Their current situation, both economic, cultural, and political, creates a sense of frustrated nationalism that gives their revisionist intent a hard edge and undermines the potential for trust with other leading powers, especially the United States.

6. Their pursuit of revisionist aims is constrained by their inherent conservatism, by the costs of major war (in particular, nuclear escalation risks), and by their dependence on the system for key national interests.

Great powers in various periods of history have shared a number of these characteristics — most centrally, a desire to tilt the playing field of world politics in their favor without upsetting the playing board altogether. But it is the particular combination of these characteristics that creates the particular challenge posed by measured revisionists — states determined to recast power balances in ways that do not risk major conflict. Such states are therefore emerging into this status looking for new techniques to expand their power. A number of dissatisfied states are actively looking for means of enhancing their influence without crossing key thresholds that would fundamentally upset the system. The gradual, unconventional approaches of gray zone strategies are giving them just such a perceived opportunity.

CHINA AS MEASURED REVISIONIST

The paradigmatic case of a measured revisionist today is China. In its identity-fueled ambitions, its determination to shift aspects of international power, and its parallel dependence on and commitment to many elements of the international rules-based order, China reflects all the paradoxical views and interests of a measured revisionist. The implication is that China is neither clearly or solely an aggressor to be deterred or a "responsible stakeholder" in the international community: It is both at the same time.

The tone of the discussion on China has been changing over the last year, with increasing emphasis on Beijing's aggressive intent. Today many, indeed perhaps most, observers see China as a more obviously revisionist actor.[18] Yet, because of the benefits it derives from the international system, Alastair Iain Johnston argued in 2003, China should not be described as a comprehensive revisionist, and his basic argument remains valid today.[19] China has boosted rather than cut back on its membership in international institutions, and arguably respected many of their core norms—such as territorial sovereignty and free trade—as well as or better than many other leading states.[20] In some cases, such as nonproliferation, it has rigorously enforced many standards and potentially violated others. The overall portrait is not of a revisionist as much as a state trying to achieve its own interests within the constraints of the system.

At the same time, in areas where China views a more direct conflict with its interests, it has rejected the norms of international institutions in selected ways. Examples include norms of human rights and military transparency, both of which China has strongly resisted. China has shifted from being a relatively passive participant in various regimes and institutions to a more active advocate of alternative organizations that better reflect its leadership, influence, and interests. An outstanding recent example of this trend is the new financial institution sponsored by Beijing—the Asian Infrastructure Development Bank. The United States urged friends and allies to shun the bank, seeing it as a barely-concealed effort to drain some of the influence from Western-led institutions like The World Bank and create a mechanism to allow Beijing to set the regional terms of development. In any event, China's initiative attracted widespread interest even from outside the region, with countries like Germany and Brazil requesting admission.[21]

Jonathan Holslag has argued that China's international involvement "does not mean that it accepts the global order." In its relations with Taiwan, for example, China is committed to a course that demands that it "profoundly change the international order and thus the balance of power." Revisionism does not demand military aggression, Holslag contends—it is "merely a desire to change the international order." In this sense, he believes that "China has been a revisionist power in a status quo guise," pursuing a strategy of "revisionism at its best: assiduous and efficient instead of noisy and antagonistic."[22] Taken together, this complex pattern of international engagement and aggressive promotion of alternative norms and institutions marks China as a measured revisionist.

China, of course, is not the only measured revisionist on the scene. Part of the argument here is that a range of rising powers, all of them responsible and peaceful members of the world community, will be increasingly viewed in this category. An especially interesting example of this category is Brazil. It reflects all the major elements of the measured revisionist category, if in less extreme and urgent ways than its more aggressive members. Brazil has more moderate ambitions surely than China or Russia but works to reform global institutions.[23] Brazil's leading political class believes that the nation deserves a greater role in world politics and has been actively seeking reform of global rules and norms to bring greater equality. Its aim is to "successfully participate in shaping the rules and forming the regimes that govern the international order."[24]

CONCLUSION

In sum, then, the international system is becoming populated with a particular type of revisionist state likely to be in the market for gray zone strategies. These states desire a shift in international distributions of power and influence, but are not tempted to go to war to get them. They are too dissatisfied and ambitious to do nothing, but too interdependent and, ultimately, responsible to become a military aggressor in classic terms. In many cases, they have turned to gray zone strategies as the cure for this dilemma. A critical aspect of such strategies, inherent to the compromise such states are making, is that they unfold gradually, over time.

ENDNOTES - CHAPTER 2

1. *The National Security Strategy of the United States of America*, Washington, DC: The White House, September 2002, transmittal letter.

2. Alastair Iain Johnston, "Is China a Status Quo Power?" *International Security,* Vol. 27, No. 4, Spring 2003, p. 8.

3. See, for example, Robert Gilpin, *War and Change in World Politics,* Cambridge, UK: Cambridge University Press, 1981, p. 34; and A. F. K. Organski and Jacek Kugler, *The War Ledger,* Chicago, IL: University of Chicago Press, 1980, pp. 1, 19-23.

4. David M. Zionts, "Revisionism and Its Variants: Understanding State Reactions to Foreign Policy Failure," *Security Studies,* Vol. 15, No. 4, October-December 2006, pp. 632-633.

5. Jason W. Davidson, "The Roots of Revisionism: Fascist Italy, 1922-39," *Security Studies,* Vol. 11, No. 4, Summer 2002, pp. 125-126.

6. Randall Schweller, "Bandwagoning for Profit: Bringing the Revisionist State Back In," *International Security,* Vol. 19, No. 1, Summer 1994, p. 87. Power transition theorists and others tend to equate revisionism to growth in power — rising states are more likely to be revisionist ones. This argument is made by power transition theorists and updated in Jason W. Davidson, "The Roots of Revisionism: Fascist Italy, 1922-39," *Security Studies,* Vol. 11, No. 4, Summer 2002, p. 128ff. The argument seems far too generic, however — there is not a reason why rising power must become revisionist.

7. Another source defines revisionist states as those "that seek to reorder an international or regional order violently"; Jason M. K. Lyall, "Paths of Ruin: Why Revisionist States Die in World Politics," draft paper, October 2006, p. 1.

8. Wolfgang Wagner, Wouter Werner, and Michael Ondero, "Rogues, Pariahs, Outlaws: Theorizing Deviance in International Relations," in Wolfgang Wagner, Wouter Werner, and Michael Ondero, eds., *Deviance in International Relations: "Rogue States" and International Security,* Basingstoke, UK: Palgrave Macmillan, 2014, p. 4. They go on to admit that "any attempt to define 'rogue states' by any set of objective criteria is doomed to fail," in large measure because no one set of characteristics will bound the sort of states the concept is trying to identify." The difficulty of capturing a single version of the concept is also discussed in K. P. O'Reilly,

"Perceiving Rogue States: The Use of the 'Rogue State' Concept by U.S. Foreign Policy Elites," *Foreign Policy Analysis*, No. 3, 2007.

9. This is the definition used by Mary Caprioli and Peter F. Trumbore, "Rhetoric vs. Reality: Rogue States in Interstate Conflict," *Journal of Conflict Resolution*, Vol. 49, No. 5, October 2005. See also Miroslav Nincic, *Renegade Regimes: Confronting Deviant Behavior in World Politics*, New York: Columbia University Press, 2005, p. 48-65.

10. Madeline Albright, "Remarks at the University of South Carolina," Columbia, SC: February 1998, available from *1997-2001.state.gov/www/statements/1998/980219c.html*.

11. George Modelski, "The Long Cycle of Global Politics and the Nation-State," *Comparative Studies in Society and History*, Vol. 20, No. 2, April 1978.

12. This point is made in Nincic, pp. 4-5, 19-23.

13. *Ibid.*, p. 2.

14. Zionts, "Revisionism and Its Variants," pp. 637-638.

15. Schweller, pp. 103-104.

16. Johnston, p. 11.

17. These categories can also be defined in the context of international relations theories. Aggressive states such as predators can be seen as responding to the logic of offensive realism — the idea that an anarchic international system mandates, or at least justifies, aggressive actions to enhance security. More moderate states including status-quo powers can be viewed as variants of "defensive realists," states who do not seek to increase their relative power and want only to be secure. One classic treatment of defensive realism is Charles L. Glaser, "Realists as Optimists: Cooperation as Self-Help," *International Security*, Vol. 19, No. 3, Winter 1994/1995. Andrew Kydd connects this argument to state type by arguing that purely security-oriented defensive states ought to be able to convey their peaceful intentions. See Andrew Kydd, "Sheep in Sheep's Clothing: Why Security Seekers Do Not Fight Each Other," *Security Studies*, Vol. 7, No. 1, Autumn 1997.

18. Aaron L. Friedberg, "The Debate Over U.S. China Strategy," *Survival*, Vol. 57, No. 3, June-July 2015, p. 102-106.

19. Johnston, pp. 12-49.

20. See, for example, Katherine Combes, "Between Revisionism and Status Quo: China In International Regimes," *POLIS*, Vol. 6, Winter 2011/2012.

21. Jane Perlez, "Stampede to Join China's Development Bank Stuns Even its Founder," *The New York Times*, April 2, 2015.

22. See Jonathan Holslag, "The Smart Revisionist," *Survival*, Vol. 56, No. 5, October-November 2014, p. 103.

23. David Rothkopf, "Brazil's New Swagger," *Foreign Policy*, February 28, 2012.

24. Harold Trinkunas, "Brazil's Rise: Seeking Influence on Global Governance," Washington, DC: The Brookings Institution Latin America Initiative, April 2014, p. 2.

CHAPTER 3

THE ADVANTAGES OF PATIENCE:
GRADUALIST CAMPAIGNS FOR ADVANTAGE

The second defining aspect of gray zone conflicts is the employment of strategic gradualism. Gray zone campaigns are designed to unfold over time rather than to gain decisive results all at once. U.S. foreign policy, always more comfortable and effective when dealing with decisive threats, needs new habits of thought to deal with this aspect of gray zone strategies.

Military strategy has often been conceived as a set of interconnected actions designed to achieve rapid, decisive results. When the United States sought to eject Saddam Hussein from Kuwait in 1990, for example, it coordinated diplomatic, economic, and military campaigns to achieve that goal in a decisive manner within a specified time period. In the most general and common-sense terms, if someone proposes to develop a "strategy" for using force to achieve a goal, the immediate impression conveyed is one of a short-term focus. We could call these "conclusive" strategies: The integration of a range of steps to achieve a decisive objective in a relatively brief period of time. The U.S. military's operational doctrines, as well, are mostly oriented to winning in the traditional phases of major combat operations.

But there is another way to approach the pursuit of national security objectives: Through a long set of interconnected actions calculated to make gradual progress.[1] Either the interests at stake are less significant, or the risk of escalation is greater, or the actor's tools are severely constrained, or some combination of all of these factors. Whatever the reason, the result is that the actor decides that the most effective way to pursue its long-term ends is not with a conclusive leap, but instead through a series of modest actions. One leading purpose of such approaches can be to avoid the sort of fundamental clash that characterizes conclusive strategies.

Evaluating the use of gradual approaches to strategy poses analytical difficulties in part because the idea overlaps with so many existing concepts, each of which has been defined somewhat differently over time. Two are especially relevant: "Salami slicing," and the use of a series of limited *faits accompli* designed to sum up to decisive effect.[2] Such gradualist approaches may also be attractive to revisionists today because such concepts tend to align with their strategic cultures: Chinese and Iranian strategic tradition recommends indirection and avoiding unnecessarily decisive fights where possible. In the strategic culture of these revisionists, the height of wisdom is not fighting a decisive, costly battle brilliantly. It is avoiding the need for such a battle in the first place while still achieving one's strategic goals. Step-by-step gray zone campaigns represent just such an approach.

THE CLASSIC THEORY: SALAMI SLICING

The gradualism I have in mind is closely analogous to the "salami-slicing" strategies discussed in Thomas Schelling's classic work, *Arms and Influence*. Schelling began his discussion of this concept with a charming metaphor. "Tell a child not to go in the water," he wrote:

> and he'll sit on the bank and submerge his feet; he is not yet "in" the water. Acquiesce, and he'll stand up;

no more of him is in the water than before. Think it over, and he'll start wading, not going any deeper; take a moment to decide whether this is different, and he'll go a little deeper, arguing that since he goes back and forth it all averages out. Pretty soon, we are calling him not to swim out of sight, wondering whatever happened to all our discipline.[3]

The problem, Schelling writes, comes from the ambiguity of commitments — the central theme in his discussion of salami slicing tactics. Even a country with a seemingly iron-clad promise to defend a border is "unlikely to start a war the first time a few drunken soldiers from the other side wander across the line and 'invade' our territory." (In the context of recent gray zone campaigns, this is exactly the problem that Ukraine faced with the initial Russian incursions of clandestine fighters.) Aggressors can thus use "tactics of erosion," testing the "seriousness of a commitment by probing it in a noncommittal way, pretending the trespass was inadvertent or unauthorized if one meets resistance." If the defender fails to respond decisively, the aggressor has set a precedent, and then moves rapidly on to the next step in the series. An aggressor can thus "begin his intrusion on too small a scale to provoke a reaction," Schelling explains, "and increase it by imperceptible degrees, never quite presenting a sudden, dramatic challenge that would invoke the committed response." Through this "steady cumulative pressure," as Schelling calls it, the aggressor eventually achieves a dramatic change in the status quo that — if they tried to bite it off all at once — would have produced a crisis, or war.[4]

The point of such tactics, in Schelling's model, is very specific — to degrade the credibility of the defender's deterrent threats. With each move that goes unpunished, the likelihood that the defender will respond the next time declines. Incremental approaches, then, carry the long-term danger of undermining the potency of promises and policies aimed at deterrence or reassurance.

An inherent danger in such approaches, as Schelling recognizes, is that an aggressor will provoke a violent response inadvertently, doing something it hopes will pass under the threshold of response, only to see it spark a massive crisis. The Soviet-North Korean invasion of the South in 1950 is one such example, an effort to use probing attacks leading to a larger intervention in the thought that the resulting ambiguity would provide the United States with the excuse it desperately wanted to stay out of the conflict. But it had the opposite effect, galvanizing not only a direct U.S. response but also a wider surge of defense spending under the aegis of National Security Council (NSC) Directive-68. This case illustrates the inherent danger of a constant stream of gradualist initiatives: They create an ever-present risk of escalation despite the desire of the aggressor to avoid them.

FAITS ACCOMPLI

A second relevant concept is the *fait accompli*, a quick, limited grab to demonstrate control before anyone can react. Political scientist Daniel Altman has investigated this particular issue in a fascinating 2015 dissertation that uses the concept as a lens to examine salami-slicing strategies. Altman views *faits accompli* as strategies designed to grab a limited gain before the other side can respond, acting suddenly and decisively in a manner that poses the defender with a dilemma of acquiescing or pursuing a dangerous escalation. Such strategies target gains small enough "that the adversary will let it go rather than escalate."[5] Like salami slicing and other gradualist approaches, of which they can be an example, *faits accomplis* aim to confront a defender with a choice between giving in and risking larger conflict.

They are not signals, because they involve an actual action which is not dependent on an opponent's concession and is designed to be nonreversible. Altman explains that:

> *Faits accomplis* take many forms in addition to seizing territory, including the construction of a nuclear reactor in violation of red lines from the international community. Most military operations are not *faits accomplis*. Military operations which do qualify include land grabs seizing territory, hostage-rescue raids like Israel's 1976 raid on Entebbe, and airstrikes to destroy weapons of mass destruction sites such as Israel's 1981 destruction of the Osirak reactor.[6]

Faits accompli need not be gradual, of course. Indeed, part of their essence is their suddenness; they are designed to be lightning strikes that achieve their goals before the defender can react. The key is the scale. An abrupt invasion that grabs half the land area of a neighboring state before anyone can respond could be a *fait accompli*, but it is far more elaborate and decisive than would be appropriate for a strategy of gradualism. On the other hand, the swift appearance of a Chinese outpost on a barren and unoccupied rock in the South China Sea can be another version of a *fait accompli* that would fit snugly into gradualist approaches: A long series of modest *faits accompli* that promote objectives over a period of time. In this regard, Russia's recent actions in Ukraine stand right at the upper bounds of gradualism, and, in fact, some would argue that they exceed it.

DEFINING STRATEGIC GRADUALISM

Building on the concepts of salami-slicing tactics, incrementalism, and *faits accompli*, gray zone campaigns can be characterized by their use of a general form of "strategic gradualism." One observer has defined gradualist strategies as involving "the slow accumulation of small changes, none of which in isolation amounts to a casus belli, but which add up over time to a substantial change in the strategic picture."[7] The goal is often not just to achieve a narrow objective, but rather to use an avalanche of incremental steps as the catalysts of an entirely new strategic reality.

Gradualist approaches are especially appealing to measured revisionists. Such states want to overturn elements of the system without causing general instability. They tend to be patient enough to take a piecemeal approach if it will help balance their mixed goals of transformation and stability. They are more willing than outright predators to surrender the speed and absoluteness of conclusive strategies for the more ambiguous and uncertain, but also less risky and escalatory, incremental approach.

At the higher end of the spectrum, gradualist strategies range from unconventional war strategies, proxy conflicts, the covert use of regular militaries, nuclear saber-rattling, wide-ranging and severe economic sanctions, and large-scale cyber activities, to far less elaborate activities at the lower end. At the more elaborate end, gradualist strategies begin to look very much like more limited conclusive ones: There is no hard-and-fast line between the two. The primary distinction is that gradualist strategies — like all elements of gray zone campaigns — are chosen specifically to avoid red lines and escalation, with a clear knowledge that they must unfold over time.

Gradualist strategies can also be designed to exploit the fissures in partnerships and alliances. The basic conundrum involved in gradualist challenges is tough enough for any one strategic actor to deal with. When the challenge is expanded to several or dozens of nations in formal or informal alliances or coalitions, each with its own distinct interests, risk appetite, and political procedures and complications, the potential for decisive or even meaningful responses to individual slices of the salami becomes almost negligible. Dealing with the gradualist approaches of both China and Russia today demonstrates this difficulty: In both cases, regional alliances or informal coalitions have had difficulty coming to consensus on the degree of threat involved in these incremental moves.

Gradualist approaches also complicate the task of deterrence and balancing. It becomes harder to recognize when a state is in direct conflict with another, for example, when conflicts unfold over time and can be difficult to identify. Such approaches create a demand for coherent long-term strategy, not merely a response to each individual event — a particularly troubling implication for the United States, which is constitutionally challenged in its ability to sustain coherent long-term efforts. Gradualism also complicates the cost-benefit calculus for specific policies, because actions appropriate to a specific imminent action can be counterproductive in the context of a long-term campaign.

Gray zone strategies, therefore, will tend to reflect these aspects of what can be called strategic gradualism. They will unfold over time, bit by bit, each step carefully remaining below clear thresholds of response. Over time, however, the architect of such a campaign intends for these incremental steps to sum up to a decisive change in the status quo. Such strategies thus involve measured revisionists acting in a deliberate and gradual manner to achieve partial revolution in the existing system. We have one major element left to examine—the tools and techniques used by such actors to build their gray zone campaigns.

ENDNOTES - CHAPTER 3

1. This is similar to the conception of Daniel Altman, who argues that traditional interstate bargaining theory focuses on relatively simple efforts to get the other side to back down—the equivalent of a conclusive strategy in a bargaining context. See Daniel Altman, "Red Lines and Faits Accomplis in Interstate Coercion and Crisis," Unpublished Ph.D. dissertation, Cambridge, MA: Massachusetts Institute of Technology, 2015, p. 18.

2. A related literature which bears on gradualist approaches is the concept of incrementalism. There is an extensive literature on incrementalism as a response to uncertainty: Decisionmakers do not feel confident enough in forecasting the results of strategic moves to make big gambles. Therefore, they proceed in small steps, tip-toeing ahead in a complex and unpredictable landscape. In a famous essay, Charles Lindblom examined the challenges of complex high-level decisions and argued that "This might be described as the method of successive limited comparisons. I will contrast it with the first approach, which might be called the rational-comprehensive method." Policy comparisons are simplified by the "limitation of policy comparisons to those policies that differ in relatively small degree from policies presently in effect." See Charles E. Lindblom, "The Science of 'Muddling Through,'" *Public Administration Review*, Vol. 19, No. 2, Spring, 1959, pp. 81, 84. Decisionmakers bite off small pieces of the problem because anything more runs into irresolvable clashes of values and interpretation.

3. Thomas C. Schelling, *Arms and Influence*, New Ed., New Haven: Yale University Press, 2008, pp. 66-67.

4. Schelling, pp. 67-68.

5. Altman, p. 21; the quote is from Glenn Snyder and Paul Diesing, *Conflict Among Nations: Bargaining, Decision Making, and System Structure in International Crises*, Princeton, NJ: Princeton Legacy Library, 2015, p. 227.

6. Altman, p. 21; the quote is from Snyder and Diesing, p. 227. Altman defines salami-slicing tactics as "repeated *faits accomplis*," though I would suggest a slightly different interpretation. A state can use many actions as a salami-slicing tactic, including, but not limited to, the specific technique of a *fait accompli*. If Russia were intent on further salami slicing in Eastern Europe, for example, it could make political claims, undertake information warfare campaigns, or offer supplies to friendly militias in countries on it periphery. All of these could be part of gradual slices of action without meeting the technical term of *fait accompli*.

7. Robert Haddick, "America Has No Answer to China's Salami-Slicing," War on the Rocks Online, February 6, 2014.

CHAPTER 4

UNCONVENTIONAL TOOLS

The third and final component of gray zone strategies involves the employment of unconventional tools of statecraft that remain below the threshold of traditional conflict. The use of such tools and techniques is hardly new. Greek city-states were employing proxy militias, fifth columnists, and early forms of information warfare several millennia ago.[1] During the Cold War, each side sought to undermine and destabilize the other without risking major conflict, and the suite of unconventional warfare (UW) measures became very elaborate. U.S. and Soviet techniques ranged from political warfare to propaganda to covert operations of every imaginable type, including support for guerrilla organizations seeking to undermine allies and proxies of the opposing superpower. Both sides developed conceptual frameworks to guide these often covert tools of statecraft, such as the Western notion of "measures short of war."[2]

States using modern gray area strategies build on this history by employing a range of tools to promote their interests and sometimes pursue their measured revisionist agendas without risking major warfare. When China sought to gain geostrategic and territorial advantages in the South China Sea, it employed a wide range of instruments of power. It backed its claims with historical narratives that spoke to its rightful mastery of large parts of the region. It approached regional states with offers of economic assistance and other carrots in exchange for cooperation. It employed civilian fishing fleets to blanket certain areas and placed oil drilling stations in key locations.

It used civilian construction companies to create new land where none had existed, and launched cyber-harassment of states that contested its claims.

Iran has wielded a similarly impressive array of unconventional, gray zone tools to bolster its influence in the Middle East and beyond. It deploys a complex and extensive network of covert operatives and quasi-military forces through its embassies and other locations. It uses energy diplomacy and the proceeds of oil riches to fund its various causes. It has a well-developed network of proxies, none more powerful than the leading hybrid warfare actor in the world—Hezbollah—to help carry out its strategic ambitions. It has taken gradual steps to build a residual nuclear capacity that offers, at a minimum, the potential for nuclear breakout if it were ever deemed necessary, as well as general geopolitical leverage.

Such tools have been discussed under the umbrella of a wide range of potential categories and issues. This category of tools and techniques has been described as a form of warfare that is unconventional, gray area, hybrid, unrestricted, untraditional, and more. Part of the challenge is to clarify this menu of concepts and, especially, to be clear about the central issue that is challenging the international system today. Three concepts in particular—hybrid warfare, UW, and political warfare—are especially useful in understanding the role of unconventional and nonmilitary elements of statecraft in making possible the new emphasis on gray zone strategies.

HYBRID WARFARE

One leading proponent of this concept, scholar Frank Hoffman, defines hybrid threats as "Any adversary that simultaneously employs a tailored mix of conventional weapons, irregular tactics, terrorism, and criminal behavior in the same time and battlespace to obtain their political objectives."[3] Hybrid conflict, he suggests, involves the employment of a broad spectrum of tactics and weapons in the same campaign, the combination of various tools — from high-end military operations to terrorism, criminality, cyberattacks, insurgency, terrorism, and more — in order to target an opponent's vulnerabilities. Hoffman has described this as "multi-modal" conflict.[4] Hybrid warfare, Hoffman continues, is characterized by "states or groups that select from the whole menu of tactics and technologies and blend them in innovative ways to meet their own strategic culture, geography, and aims."[5]

Defined this way, hybrid warfare would seem to be a very broad and encompassing concept, more than expansive enough to include gray zone strategies. Indeed, the North Atlantic Treaty Organization has officially used this term to describe Russian actions in Ukraine.[6] Most commonly however, commentators have used the term "hybrid warfare" to refer to combinations of conventional and unconventional means designed to produce or lay the groundwork for eventual decisive operations by military forces. It is not a gray area tactic in itself so much as the appendage of gray area tactics to major war.[7]

Hybrid warfare marries conventional military operations, either sequentially or in parallel, to a range of other tactics largely built around psychological operations and information warfare. The goal is to target the opinion of publics in states waging war, both to reinforce the commitment of friendly publics and destroy the morale of adversaries. Most hybrid approaches also point to strategies that integrate guerrilla and other irregular operations with conventional ones.[8]

The result is a cross-boundary military effort that integrates many different forms of competition and conflict into a cohesive whole. But, again, the purpose of hybrid warfare is either to win a conclusive campaign through the use of force and some level or violence, or else to set the stage for some sort of decisive military action, perhaps through combined arms operations. Hybrid warfare is closer to a variety of conventional warfare than a true alternative to it.

In another article, Hoffman makes clear the limitations of his hybrid concept. "The problem with the hybrid threats definition," he wrote:

> is that it focuses on combinations of tactics associated with violence and warfare (except for criminal acts) but completely fails to capture other non-violent actions. Thus, it does not address instruments including economic and financial acts, subversive political acts like creating or covertly exploiting trade unions and NGOs as fronts, or information operations using false websites and planted newspaper articles. It also fails to address what a pair of Chinese Army Colonels discussed in their book titled *Unrestricted Warfare* (really *War without Borders*) that was explicitly critical of Western and American conceptions of war. That concept included diplomatic and financial and information tools as part of a larger conception of warfare.[9]

Hybrid warfare, then, in Hoffman's sense, still refers to the employment of tools and techniques of violence to achieve political ends — but tools that mix approaches from forms of types of warfare often thought distinct, such as decisive action and irregular war. Such operations overlap with the higher-intensity end of gray zone conflict as I am defining it, but the hybrid warfare concept clearly imagines a far more violent clash that involves direct use of many military instruments. In this sense, hybrid war is truly "war" in a Clausewitzian sense, whereas gray zone strategies are a less violent and looser form of conflict.

UNCONVENTIONAL WARFARE

A number of the tactics and techniques being employed in gray zone strategies overlap with classic UW. The term often is used to apply to a wide range of activities, but its technical definition refers, as David Maxwell has made clear, to efforts to support foreign insurgencies. He cites the official Department of Defense (DoD) definition, which characterizes UW as "activities to enable a resistance movement or insurgency to coerce, disrupt or overthrow a government or occupying power through and with an underground, auxiliary, and guerrilla force in a denied area."[10] A number of early discussions also include political terrorism in service of insurgent campaigns in this category.

Greek city-states engaged in long-running campaigns of subversion against each other using all manner of proxy and insurgent forces, including fomenting slave rebellions. The Romans made extensive use of UW in connection with hundreds of proxy forces throughout its empire.[11] In the modern era, UW perhaps reached its heyday in World War II and the Cold War that followed. Such operations were common in World War II, as in Allied operations to disrupt the German occupation of Yugoslavia.[12] During the Cold War, Moscow employed a range of UW strategies in various theaters as part of its general approach to subversion.[13] The United States and its allies used UW just as energetically to undermine Communist rule from Afghanistan to Eastern Europe.

The concept of UW is making a comeback in a context where major powers desire to avoid direct confrontation, while engaging in competition and rivalry over important but ultimately secondary interests. In both Afghanistan and Iraq, senior leaders in DoD—both within the policy process and to the general public—advertised the operations as UW campaigns, involving U.S. support for local proxies more than direct application of U.S. conventional military might.[14] Russia's gray zone strategies in the Caucasus and Eastern Europe have also made liberal use of guerrilla tactics and local proxy forces.

POLITICAL WARFARE

A closely related category is sometimes referred to as "political warfare." It involves measures to promote fragmentation and instability on the home front or within the military of an opposing power. Some recent descriptions of gray zone forms of conflict have employed the term "political warfare" to describe some of what has taken place in Eastern Europe and elsewhere: Russia's cyber campaign against Estonia in 2007, for example, was designed in part to convey political messages about the inability of Estonia's government to safeguard its citizens.

In one sense, all of gray zone conflict represents a form of political warfare. Its goal is to employ a range of tools of statecraft to achieve specific political objectives. Its activities are integrated tightly into political realities and dynamics, and it can only work if it succeeds in molding political realities and perceptions in the intended way. Gray zone conflict, then, **is** political warfare to a great degree. But there are specific ways in which the more directly politically-oriented tools of such campaigns can be understood as a discrete category of effort.

George F. Kennan's famous invocation of "measures short of war" laid out a range of diplomatic, political, economic, and other aspects of broad national security strategy. During the Cold War, the Soviet Union employed what it called "active measures," political, economic, and social subversion designed to weaken the West and clear the way for the victory of socialism. The key difference was that these measures would be used consistently to work out rivalry between "great centers of power and ideology in this world" — measures used for the "promulgation of power."[15] Kennan was discussing a context of persistent competition, rather than one in which states could resolve their disputes and move on to another issue. "Political warfare," Kennan argued, "is the logical application of Clausewitz's doctrine in time of peace."

> In broadest definition, political warfare is the employment of all the means at a nation's command, short of war, to achieve its national objectives. Such operations are both overt and covert. They range from such overt actions as political alliances, economic measures (as ERP — the Marshall Plan), and "white" propaganda to such covert operations as clandestine support of "friendly" foreign elements, "black" psychological warfare and even encouragement of underground resistance in hostile states."[16]

The strategic coherence of U.S. Cold War political warfare can be exaggerated,[17] but the approach was certainly at the center of both U.S. and Soviet Cold War strategies. The reason, moreover, was somewhat similar to the basis for the current surge in interest — the desire to avoid direct confrontation.

The primary importance of political warfare today is in terms of integrated strategies bringing together information operations, development aid, regime support, and other nonviolent options to encourage specific political outcomes. Some have argued for a political warfare concept at the heart of the global contest with violent extremism.[18] China has arguably been waging versions of political warfare in its campaigns for influence in Africa and Asia.

CONCLUSION

These three concepts give some flavor of the sort of unconventional, cross-boundary set of tools and techniques that can be employed in gray zone conflict. They can be integrated into holistic, gradual campaigns to achieve political ends. Such tools appear to be of particular interest to measured revisionists, states determined to reframe global balance of power but equally committed to achieving that goal without major war and, in fact, without even losing their status as a recognized member of the rules-based international order.

In these ambitions, such powers are aided by the development of a wide range of gray zone concepts, approaches, and technologies that provide multiple avenues to pursue limited revisionist intent without risking major war. Many of these have been on display in recent years — actions from economic sanctions and energy diplomacy to cyberattacks to information operations to generate revisionist narratives to sponsorship of militias and fifth columnists to the aggressive use of nonmilitary forces such as coast guards. Such tools and techniques are not new. But the sum total of their effect has become unprecedented, and offers peaceful revisionists a meaningful avenue to their goals without outright conflict.

The combination of these three elements—measured revisionism, strategic gradualism, and unconventional tools and techniques—together account for the origins and character of gray zone conflict. The report turns now to a more detailed assessment of that concept.

ENDNOTES - CHAPTER 4

1. See, for example, Dave Coughran, "Another Way to Fight: Unconventional Warfare from Rome to Iran," *Harvard Kennedy School Review*, May 2, 2013, available from *harvardkennedyschoolreview.com/another-way-to-fight-unconventional-warfare-from-rome-to-iran/*.

2. John J. Tierney, *Chasing Ghosts: Unconventional Warfare in American History*, Washington, DC: Potomac Books, 2006, focuses to a large extent on guerrilla tactics but is a fascinating and impressive survey.

3. Cited in Frank Hoffman, "On Not-So-New Warfare: Political Warfare vs. Hybrid Threats," *War on the Rocks*, July 28, 2014, available from *warontherocks.com/2014/07/on-not-so-new-warfare-political-warfare-vs-hybrid-threats/*.

4. Frank N. Hoffman, "Hybrid Threats: Reconceptualizing the Evolving Character of Modern Conflict," Washington, DC: National Defense University *Strategic Forum* No. 240, April 2009, 5.

5. Other defining recent works on hybrid war include William J. Nemeth, "Future War and Chechnya: A Case for Hybrid Warfare," Thesis submitted to the Naval Postgraduate School, June 2002, available from *calhoun.nps.edu/bitstream/handle/10945/5865/02Jun_Nemeth.pdf?sequence=1*; Colonel John J. McCuen, "Hybrid Wars," *Military Review*, March-April 2008; and Frank Hoffman, *Conflict in the 21st Century: The Rise of Hybrid Wars*, Arlington, VA: Potomac Institute, December 2007.

6. "Hybrid War, Hybrid Response," Washington, DC: North Atlantic Treaty Organization, July 3, 2014.

7. Deputy Secretary of Defense Robert Work made this distinction in his 2015 U.S. Army War College speech, arguing that "as difficult and as challenging as the gray zone will be, it will pale in comparison when that type of conflict then escalates from the shadowy actions of 'fifth-columnists' and 'little green men,' to state-sponsored and state-directed hybrid proxy war."

8. A good summary is András Ràcz, *Russia's Hybrid War in Ukraine*, Helsinki, Finland: The Finnish Institute of International Affairs, June 2015, pp. 28-34.

9. Hoffman, "On Not-So-New Warfare."

10. David Maxwell, "Do We Really Understand Unconventional War?" *Small Wars Journal*, October 23, 2014. See also Mark Grdovic, "Developing a Common Understanding of Unconventional Warfare," *Joint Force Quarterly*, Issue 57, Second Quarter, 2010.

11. Coughran, "Another Way to Fight."

12. J. Darren Duke, Rex L. Phillips, and Christopher J. Conover, "Challenges in Coalition Unconventional Warfare: The Allied Campaign in Yugoslavia, 1941-1945," *Joint Force Quarterly*, Fourth Quarter 2014.

13. For early discussions of these tactics, see Raymond L. Garthoff, "Unconventional War in Communist Strategy," *Foreign Affairs*, July 1962; Franklin A. Lindsay, "Unconventional Warfare," *Foreign Affairs*, Vol. 40, No. 2, January 1962; and Andrew C. Janos, "Unconventional Warfare: Framework and Analysis," *World Politics*, Vol. 15, No. 4, July 1963.

14. Hy Rothstein has argued that these claims were somewhat misleading, and that both campaigns relied much more on conventional military power than would a true UW campaign. See Hy Rothstein, *Afghanistan and the Troubled Future of Unconventional Warfare*, Newport, RI: U.S. Naval Institute Press, 2006.

15. George F. Kennan, *Measures Short of War: The George F. Kennan Lectures at the National War College, 1946-1947*, Washington, DC: National Defense University Press, 1991, pp. 4-5.

16. George Kennan, Policy Planning Staff Memorandum, "The Inauguration of Organized Political Warfare," May 4, 1948, available from *academic.brooklyn.cuny.edu/history/johnson/65ciafounding3.htm*.

17. Scott Lucas and Kaeten Mistry, "Illusions of Coherence: George F. Kennan, U.S. Strategy and Political Warfare in the Early Cold War, 1946–1950," *Diplomatic History*, Vol. 33, No. 1, January 2009.

18. Donovan C. Chau, "Political Warfare: An Essential Instrument of U.S. Strategy Today," *Comparative Strategy*, Vol. 25, No. 2, 2006.

CHAPTER 5

UNDERSTANDING GRAY ZONE CONFLICT

Gray zone conflict therefore reflects the collision of three major trends in world politics: The limited but nonetheless transformative intentions of measured revisionists; the reliance on incremental approaches to revise elements of the system one bite at a time; and the employment of nontraditional tools of statecraft to achieve gradual but decisive results in the no-man's-land between peace and war. The result is a pattern of state rivalry that can substitute for traditional military aggression, and which can pose serious challenges to U.S. strategy.

At the same time, however, there are powerful constraints on the effectiveness of these approaches, and they can easily become counterproductive. As we will see, as much as gray zone strategies attempt to escape significant retaliation by staying "under the radar" of key thresholds, they do not always succeed. Both China and Russia have prompted serious blowback with their gray zone efforts. There may be a real dilemma at the core of such strategies: They can either avoid meaningful response or achieve significant and timely results, but they have difficulty doing both.

THE MOTIVE: THE RISKS OF MAJOR WAR, AND RELATIVE WEAKNESS

The growing importance of gray zone strategies does not assume that full-scale armed aggression has become impossible. But the costs of large-scale aggression have become severe while the potential benefits have declined, and it has simply ceased to be a meaningful option for nearly all states nearly all the time.[1] Warfare between major powers in Europe, Asia, or the Middle East remains entirely plausible, but, if it occurs, it is likely to emerge through some combination of accident, miscalculation, and misperception rather than because of the conscious choice of a national leadership. The trend is more than theoretical: Extensive recent empirical work indicates that the incidence and severity of major war has declined significantly over the last century, and projects that, absent possible shocks to the system, it is likely to continue to do so.[2]

This monograph has identified a number of specific reasons why outright aggression will only serve a state's interests under exceptionally narrow conditions. Territorial aggression promises to be more costly than ever before, partly because of the risk of nuclear escalation but also because of the role of media and the combination of advanced insurgent tactics and technologies of resistance. The value of aggression has declined at a time when states can acquire what they need through trade, and when the relative importance of such territorially-based prizes as minerals and raw materials is not what it once was. Aggressors risk being shunned by the international community and ejected from the economic, technological, and social networks essential to national prosperity. Leading interest groups in major states view their own stakes as bound up with peace and stability and oppose measures that would threaten those values. Of course, when an opponent is a nuclear power or allied to one, the risk of national devastation outweighs any potential advantage that could be gained from adventurism.[3]

Yet rivalry, aggression, and frustration with existing distributions of goods and power hardly have disappeared from the map of world politics. Many states still view key neighbors with suspicion and even hatred. Security dilemmas remain as real today as they have been throughout the history of the state system. Rivalry will continue in different ways, and Nadia Schadlow has argued for attention to "the space between peace and war" as a critical future trend in world politics. The battlegrounds in these conflicts revolve around the information environment and perceptions, and states try to gain the upper hand with coercive actions short of large-scale military use.[4]

In the meantime, many states can also be attracted to gray zone techniques because of their relative weakness. Russian and Chinese gray zone tactics lately have been interpreted as indications of cunning and influence, when, in fact, they may speak to a fundamental inability to do anything more.[5] Russia's economic weakness may mean that it simply cannot acquire a conventional military of sufficient strength to pursue its regional goals, leaving it to turn to gray zone campaigns as an alternative. Mark Galeotti has pointedly observed that Russia, "a country with an economy somewhere between the size of Italy's and Brazil's is seeking to assert a great power international role and agenda." He uses the phrase "guerrilla geopolitics" to characterize the resulting attraction to gray zone strategies: Russia is trying to punch above its weight, and shifting to major combat would expose at least some of its vulnerabilities.[6] For China, Russia, Iran, and others, operating in the gray zone allows them to dampen the relative power differences between them and the United States and its allies. In this sense, gray zone strategies are a form of asymmetric tool, a sort of multi-instrument insurgency.

DEFINING GRAY ZONE CONFLICT

In this context, gray zone conflict might be understood as having a number of characteristics. It could be considered as a form of conflict that:

- Pursues political objectives through cohesive, integrated campaigns;
- Employs mostly nonmilitary or nonkinetic tools;
- Strives to remain under key escalatory or red line thresholds to avoid outright, conventional conflict; and,
- Moves gradually toward its objectives rather than seeking conclusive results in a specific period of time.

An important distinction regarding such means of conflict is whether states actively and consciously **choose** gray zone strategies as an alternative to other forms of seeking their political objectives. In some cases, states experimenting with gray zone techniques are really developing variations on the theme of traditional combat—things like asymmetric war, which involve open fighting if in irregular ways, or limited war, which involves outright combat pursued with mutually-agreed constraints.[7] Or they could be using gray zone campaigns as a prelude to potential warfare, rather than an alternative to it. Relatively weak states may grab at gray zone tools and techniques, not because they consider this set of options a unique and coherent strategic concept, but because they have no choice. This monograph argues that we see some evidence that states have indeed embraced gray zone strategies as a distinct and specific form of conflict, but that evidence remains inconclusive.

Figure 5-1 lays out a range of tools and techniques that can be used to assemble gray-zone campaigns. These lists are in no way meant to be comprehensive; they are suggestive and illustrative of the sort of actions available to measured revisionists. These are tools that in one way or another tend to fit well into gray zone approaches. None is necessarily designed to achieve a rapid victory in the sense of the classic use of military force.

	Economic	Military / Clandestine	Informational	Political	Other
High End	• Blockade • Severe sanctions • Energy coercion	• Nuclear posturing • Movements of troops, threats • Creation of fait accompli situations • Large-scale covert actions to weaken regime • Discrete acts of violence at key moments • Use of UW forces (SOF, covert operators) in direct action with deniability • Sponsoring large scale proxy violence	• Major propaganda campaigns • Large-scale deception and denial to conceal revisionist intent	• Support for domestic opposition, exiles, guerrillas, militias • Major claims in global forums to support revisionist intent; urgent efforts to change rules, distribution of goods • Conclude formal alliances • Sign treaties	• Large scale cyberattacks • Use of nonmilitary assets (coast guard, fishing fleets) to create de facto presence
Middle Ground	• Targeted sectoral denial • Limited sanctions	• Large-scale exercises • Signaling • Moderate covert actions for leverage or specific goals • Sponsoring moderate proxy activities • Expand/revise military presence in regions/states	• Develop and publicize historical narrative • Moderate propaganda campaign	• Dialogues with adversary political opposition • Moderate efforts in international forums to revise rules • Establish regional concerts	• Cyberharassing, targeted cyber actions
Low End	• Trade policies • Implied economic coercion	• Small-scale covert actions for modest goals • Low-level backing for proxy attacks	• General information diplomacy	• Use of global forums to assert goals on persistent basis • Networks, Track 2 efforts	• Low-level, ongoing cyber activities

Figure 5-1. Gray Zone Tools and Techniques.

A given gradualist campaign could involve a whole mosaic of actions assembled from this broad menu. The key to a gray zone campaign is not so much the tools—though by definition they will remain short of high-intensity conflict—as much as the phased and incremental way they are employed, and the fact that the campaign is seeking to achieve political goals short of major war rather than laying the groundwork for, or supporting the conduct of, combined-arms operations.

Such strategies could then involve a range of possible actions, captured in Figure 5-2. These can range from peacetime cooperation to competition to low-level gradualism to moderate to high-level, as in Russia. A number of these approaches could be combined into an overall campaign, and the intensity can be modulated depending on the interests at stake or the risk tolerance of the aggressing state.

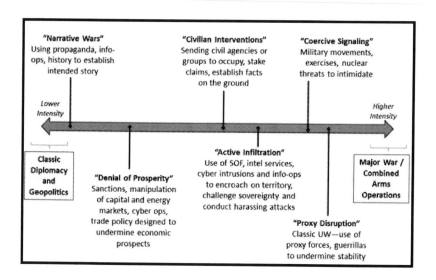

Figure 5-2. A Spectrum of Gray Zone Techniques.

Nuclear weapons can also support gray zone strategies in a number of specific ways. By definition, these strategies are designed to stay under key thresholds, to force the choice of escalation onto the defender and ideally achieve intended political objectives without resort to major combat. In the process, nuclear weapons can help to insulate gray zone campaigns by raising the perceived risk of escalation. Russia, for example, has undertaken many avenues of gray zone aggression — all the while making explicit reference to its potential willingness to use nuclear weapons to defend interests it identifies as vital. The effect is to magnify the dangers of escalation for the other side, and clear the way for Russia's gray zone actions. Indeed, a number of strategic capabilities and threats — cyber and long-range conventional strike as well as nuclear weapons — can play this role in gray zone campaigns.

OPERATING BELOW THRESHOLDS, CREATING DILEMMAS

The central strategic concept of gray zone strategies is to confront their targets with a conundrum. Any one specific act in the chain will have limited stakes, but responding to it has the potential to escalate and create a crisis. One source uses the terminology of salami-slicing gradualism to build an argument that applies to gray zone strategies more generally:

> Policymakers in Washington will be caught in a bind attempting to apply this military power against an accomplished salami-slicer. If sliced thinly enough, no one action will be dramatic enough to justify starting a war. How will a policymaker in Washington justify drawing a red line in front of a CNOOC oil rig anchoring inside Vietnam's EEZ [exclusive economic zone],

or a Chinese frigate chasing off a Philippines survey ship over Reed Bank, or a Chinese infantry platoon appearing on a pile of rocks near the Spratly Islands? When contemplating a grievously costly war with a major power, such minor events will appear ridiculous as *casus belli*. Yet when accumulated over time and space, they could add up to a fundamental change in the region.[8]

Despite the risks and complications of responding, therefore, ignoring the gradual steps allows the aggressor at least in theory to progressively change the strategic landscape in important ways. Gradual gray zone tactics are thus designed to place their intended targets in a no-win position: "It is the rivals of salami-slicers who are obligated to eventually draw red lines and engage in brinkmanship over actions others will view, in isolation, as trivial and far from constituting *casus belli*."[9]

A fundamental implication of gray zone campaigns is to blur the dividing line between peace and war, and between civilian and military endeavors. They are, in a sense, the use of civilian instruments to achieve objectives sometimes reserved for military capabilities. They place all of society at risk and create a sense of ongoing conflict, even if not through the deployment of traditional military formations to seize territory. Gray zone campaigns thus continue the tendency of various forms of conflict — terrorism, insurgency, and nuclear threats included — to make civilian populations a regular target.[10]

Conflict or War?

Although it is a form of persistent conflict and a means of achieving state objectives through force, gray zone conflict can be distinguished from "warfare" as classically defined—a distinction that suggests the need for a new theory of gray zone conflict. In his initial and perhaps most famous definition, for example, Carl von Clausewitz writes that "War is thus an act of force to compel our enemy to do our will."[11] If this were as far as Clausewitz got, gray zone conflict might qualify as warfare, depending on how one defined "force." But in many places, Clausewitz clearly understands war in traditional terms: As military forces applying violence in defined engagements to win a discrete victory.[12] When he does refer to the potential to defeat an enemy through delaying tactics and the gradual imposition of costs, he clearly seems to have in mind violent means of doing so with military forces. More commonly, when referring to the requirements for victory, he speaks of traditional outcomes: Destroying enemy forces, "disarming" the enemy, seizing their capital, undermining their will through the application of violence, all designed to achieve a decisive victory on the battlefield. When thinking of war, Clausewitz had in mind what we would consider to be major combat operations: The employment of military forces to achieve a decisive victory on the battlefield.

As often as he reminds his readers that war is **not** a distinct and separate activity, but merely the "continuation of policy by other means,"[13] Clausewitz also takes pains to stress the ways in which the environment of war **is** unique. War is a distinctive enterprise with particular characteristics—violence, fear, passion and emotion, chance, and friction. Crossing the threshold into a situation of war is a momentous decision that must be understood as a departure from regular life, the inauguration of a different context, with different rules and realities.

In all of these senses, gray zone conflict cannot be understood as war. It does not usually involve violence or bloodshed, at least not as its essential approach. It does not aim at clearly defined engagements, and there is no identifiably distinct battlefield. It is not conducted primarily by military forces, or, at a minimum, their activities are nested deeply into a more integrated campaign directed by civilians.

Gray zone conflict involves the holistic application of a mosaic of civilian and military tools, short of combat operations, to achieve gradual progress toward political objectives. It therefore does reflect Clausewitz's core dictum about war—it is another way of conceiving "the continuation of policy by other means." But it reflects such a continuation through a very different approach than Clausewitz would have understood as warfare. It is a distinct form of the use of force—social, economic, political, and informational as well as military force—to achieve objectives.[14] It creates a blended version of conflict by blurring the boundary between peace and war, and civilian and military tools and categories.

One might think that Sun Tzu, the military theorist often contrasted with Clausewitz, would offer a concept of conflict more aligned to gray zone efforts. But, in fact, Sun Tzu understands war, ultimately, in much the same way as Clausewitz does—as the use of military forces in engagements for the purposes of decisive victory. The *Art of War* speaks in terms of the use of armies, "troops," force, and violence to gain territory and crush adversary forces. It argues that generals work best when left alone by political leaders, hardly a recipe for an integrated civil-military campaign. It demands speed, and has little tolerance for gradual operations. "We have not yet seen a clever operation that was prolonged."[15]

Some might find support for gray zone approaches in Sun Tzu's well-known injunction that winning battles is not the key to success: "To subdue the enemy without fighting is the acme of skill." But Sun Tzu's dominant view, as illustrated in dozens of comments throughout the work, is that this is achieved by maneuvering and placement of armed forces, deception, some degree of clandestine operations — to "defeat their strategy" as Sun Tzu urges — rather than through operations lower on the spectrum of force. It is an army that is taking these actions, not a range of civilian capabilities.[16] Avoiding battle is about using military strategy to affect enemy perceptions in the context of a face-off of military force.

From the standpoint of classic military theory, then, gray zone conflict does not meet the traditional criteria for warfare. Its character and challenge will be specific to its nature, and must be thought of differently than war itself. This fact has a number of implications. One is that the principles governing the conduct of conventional warfare need to be modified, and in some cases abandoned, when conceiving of a doctrine for gray zone conflict.

A second and equally important implication has to do with the legal implications of gray zone conflict. The United Nations (UN) Charter prohibits "armed attack" on a neighbor, in service of UN overarching goal of preventing "breaches of the peace." Because they do not reflect unambiguous use of force, gray zone techniques can create significant challenges from an international legal standpoint. It is not clear, for example, whether these coercive and often aggressive actions meet the standard of "armed attack" and therefore allow retaliatory action under Article 51's guarantee of self-defense. In a controversial 1985 decision, the International Court of Justice ruled that Nicaraguan meddling in El Salvador did not generate a self-defense situation, and held that U.S. support for the contras violated international law.[17] One goal of gray zone strategies is to remain below this particular threshold and thus not furnish defending states with a rationale for retaliation that is legal under international law.

States engaged in gray zone conflicts, therefore, are not technically "at war." The permissions and protections of many international agreements that reference wartime, from the UN Charter to the Geneva Conventions, do not apply to gray zone contexts. The last 15 years have been a continual reminder of the great challenges of conducting quasi-wartime activities in a context that does not, in many critical ways, qualify as war. Because gray zone conflicts can last for years — perhaps even decades — exceptions to normal social or political norms will be much more challenging to sustain. As they do with the political context, then, gray zone campaigns create a vague, ambiguous environment for legal standards and judgment.

A third challenge is that, in a gray zone conflict, it can be difficult or impossible to define "victory." The goals of traditional warfare are typically clear, the definition of success or victory is self-evident, and once one side has "won," it is obvious to everyone. In gray zone campaigns, however, a clear concept of victory can be elusive. For China, the day when all other regional powers accede to Beijing's claims of sovereignty over key components of the South China Sea would represent an unambiguous signal of victory. But such a day, in such unequivocal terms, is never likely to arrive: There will be no "surrender ceremony" with other states signing a document abandoning their claims. Instead, the campaign is likely to persist for years, generating occasionally clear advances, frequent reversals, and no final objective outcomes. The same will be true for the United States and allied responses to such campaigns.

We can already see the challenges of waging such conflicts for U.S. and friendly democratic states. Such societies are more comfortable with simple, traditional conflicts with well-defined objectives, a defined time frame, and a clear winner. Operating a changing, ambiguous, long-term campaign challenges the strategic personality of democracies. Because so many elements of gray zone strategies operate in the shadows — secret and clandestine activities — running such campaigns can undermine public oversight of foreign and national security policy.

At the same time, one lesson is that states employing gray zone campaigns may find themselves frustrated in their ability to achieve objectives in measurable ways. Patience and a measured, long-term approach are appealing until they fail to generate progress. Indeed, one lesson of recent and historic experience may be that gray zone campaigns often simply do not work, or will be perceived as failing given the political pressures weighing on national leaderships at critical moments. They could then set the stage for an escalation if a state views the desired objective as a vital interest.

Limitations, Constraints, and Dilemmas.

Gray zone strategies are not perfect, and they do not always achieve the goals laid out for them. In fact, they can become counterproductive: If pursued aggressively enough, they will generate some of the same backlash and counterbalancing as traditional military campaigns. When considering the potential danger posed by such tactics, it is important to recognize their weaknesses as well as strengths.

To begin with, gray zone strategies simply can fail to achieve the broader political goals laid out for them. Unlike traditional military operations, they do not involve decisive moves to achieve specific outcomes. They creep up on their goals gradually—but that process can be interrupted or countered. China's series of actions in the South China Sea, for example, can only go so far without the forcible annexation of certain land masses. It might never prompt other countries in the region to accept Beijing's territorial claims. Gray zone strategies represent a sort of compromise for their authors, generating less risk than outright aggression but also reflecting a less decisive form of action and less guarantee of success.

The potential for gray zone progress, moreover, depends at least partly on the degree to which the intended targets are able to respond in kind. To the extent that Vietnam, the Philippines, Japan, and other targets of China's gray zone efforts build their own capabilities in these areas—generating counternarratives, using information campaigns to promote their version of events, deploying expanded civilian maritime capabilities to the area, actively subverting China's efforts through such means as harassment and cyber actions—the result could be a gray zone stalemate rather than gradual Chinese progress. Like any other strategy, efforts in the gray zone can be matched and countered.

Indeed, in the long-run, if the set of international norms, rules, and institutions that has been building up since 1945 remains largely intact, the authors of aggressive gray zone strategies may be at a disadvantage in such contests. The main advantage of such approaches is to achieve strategic advantage while remaining below certain thresholds for response. It is now clear, however, that gray zone campaigns being undertaken by China, Russia, and Iran are in fact generating significant concern and reaction—in part because they are viewed as violating key norms of conduct widely respected in the world community. In order to press its gray zone campaign effectively, for example, China must refuse binding negotiations to settle its maritime claims in international institutions—it might not get the outcome it wants. In choosing gray zone aggression over formal talks, though, China identifies itself as an aggressor and a state unwilling to play by the rules of international politics.

There may be something of a dilemma for the architects of gray zone strategies, then, a mirror-image of the dilemma such strategies try to impose on their victims. It may be that gray zone strategies can be either powerful enough to achieve real progress, or stealthy enough to fall so far below thresholds of response that they generate no effective counteraction—but not both. If a gray zone strategy is powerful enough to make real progress toward significant political goals, it is likely to threaten norms of international conduct, and thus fail in its central goal of avoiding a meaningful response. This is certainly the pattern we see in Asia, Europe, and the Middle East today.

This dilemma points to the major risk of gray zone strategies: That they will reveal their authors as clandestine adventurists and provoke powerful and even escalatory responses. Many analyses of gray zone strategies seem to assume that states which confront them cannot or will not take decisive or even meaningful steps to respond, that they will be lulled into a sense of security and fearful that any response will escalate into conflict. There has been some of this flavor in the West's response to Russian gray zone aggression in Eastern Europe, to be sure, and there is little question that such techniques do pose a serious challenge for U.S. and allied national security strategies. But Russia's actions have prompted serious countermoves, as have China and Iran's—from arming alternative proxies to diplomatic campaigns to economic sanctions to military deployments and exercises.

The risk of escalation, moreover, is ever-present, and could confront the authors of gray zone strategies with outcomes for which they are ill-prepared. As we have seen, gray zone approaches might be properly understood as strategies of the weak, states that might theoretically consider more direct military action but which are not confident of their ability to prevail. Escalation would bring them into a perilous domain, one with significant dangers of military failure. Gray zone strategies generate a constant risk of such escalation by creating an atmosphere of contention and zero-sum rivalry and a sense of a state trying to impose its will through force. They also tend to involve a long series of provocative, sometimes violent actions which could spark a larger dispute at any moment: Run-ins between Chinese and U.S. vessels and aircraft and the pro-Russian Ukrainian militia's shoot-down of a civilian airliner are leading examples of such potential triggers. Gray zone strategies are not like steady diplomatic campaigns: They are forceful, destabilizing, and operate constantly on the knife-edge of escalation to the sort of outright conflict their authors want to avoid.

It is also worth noting that gray zone strategies are not cost-free. Russia's campaign in Eastern Europe, for example, must entail significant direct costs: The operational expenses of its major military actions; funds delivered to proxies; and specific capabilities built for such campaigns. There is no reliable estimate of the cost of such a campaign, but it is likely to run into the billions, creating an opportunity cost of other activities or capabilities foregone. Even more substantially, both Iran and Russia have faced stiff economic sanctions as a result of their efforts to achieve advantage in the gray zone: Again, even restrained aggression contravenes international norms and can provoke punishments. By all accounts, these sanctions have done serious damage to Russian and Iranian economies. Finally, there is the geopolitical cost of being identified as an aggressor—the cooperation foregone, the potential friends alienated, the counterbalancing provoked.

In sum, then, while gray zone strategies represent a notable threat to U.S. and allied interests, their potential should not be overestimated. They have important limits and constraints. Russia and Iran are almost certainly **worse** off today—economically, geopolitically, and militarily—because of the costs of and reactions to their gray zone campaigns. China is already paying a significant price for its gray zone adventurism. The following recommendations are designed to build on this fundamental insight—that gray zone strategies require their authors to challenge international norms and can easily generate powerful counter-campaigns even as they remain under given thresholds. An effective response would build on this reality and use international norms, rules and institutions as the basis for punishing and deterring would-be gray zone aggressors.

THE CHALLENGE TO U.S. STRATEGY

Despite their limitations and risks, carefully developed gray zone strategies pose a serious challenge to U.S. national security strategy. This is true for a number of reasons. First, U.S. foreign policy tends to be more comfortable with broad and simple principles — blunt warnings for specific actions and unconditional commitments. The U.S. global role, moreover, is most legitimate when acting in defense of clear norms or principles that have been unquestionably violated by some revisionist power. The United States is more often confounded when it confronts ill-defined, seemingly innocuous actions by revisionist challengers working to furnish themselves with genuine legal and political validation.

These factors reinforce the basic dilemma that gradualist approaches are trying to engineer. As Daniel Altman has argued, if deterring the first *fait accompli* fails, how do states prevent being taken apart piece by piece with salami tactics? "Making credible the threat to retaliate is essential for deterrence, but it is no easy task when the stakes are limited."[18]

From an operational perspective, as well, the U.S. military tends to focus on the major combat aspects of campaigns — the "Phase III" component, as it has been known over the last decade and a half. U.S. operational doctrine, force structure and technologies are designed and procured in order to prevail once Phase III kicks off. As has been demonstrated repeatedly in recent conflicts, the U.S. military tends to assume that the pre-war and post-war contexts are someone else's responsibility. Pre-war actions are generally limited to "preparing the battlefield," actions designed strictly to improve U.S. performance in the main fight.

Steven Metz has catalogued a number of aspects of U.S. strategic culture that make it temperamentally unsuited to fighting gray zone conflicts. "America is organizationally and psychologically unprepared for unrestricted warfare," he has argued:

> Washington's instinct is to compartmentalize the elements of power and apply them in sequence, first trying diplomacy and phone calls, treating crises as if they are simply a big misunderstanding. . . . The entire American strategic culture, ethos and security organization is diametric to unrestricted warfare. The United States wants its conflicts and security problems to remain tidily restricted. Its strength is greatest when there is no political ambiguity or ethical confusion, and when partners jump on board. This is precisely why America's adversaries will not fight this way.[19]

The United States often appears to display frustration with gray zone strategies, as if they are somehow violating norms of international conduct. In a way, they are — gray zone aggressors are seeking to reshape international norms and meddle with the rule-based order in ways that the United States will find both threatening and underhanded. Moreover, the persistence and aggressive character of such actions is characteristic of an era of growing rivalry and competition among leading powers that runs against the U.S. narrative of leading states with largely aligned interests seeking stability.

The challenge today is to develop a mindset and a national security strategy appropriate to an era of mixed or paradoxical trends. What seems to be emerging is a period of rivalry alongside cooperation on shared interests, fierce ideological competition alongside a deepening global commitment to basic cosmopolitan goals, national strategies that respect the value of a rule-based order, and yet use gray zone tactics that threaten elements of that order. All of this points to the need for complex, nuanced, sometimes contradictory approaches to promote global stability at a time of growing tension.

ENDNOTES - CHAPTER 5

1. Any broad conclusion such as this will have to admit exceptions, and the concept of the infeasibility of large-scale aggression is no different. The U.S. invasion of Iraq could be said to be an outlier, for example.

2. One recent example is the *Global Defense Outlook 2015*, Deloitte, 2015, pp. 10-12.

3. This is not merely a theoretical conclusion. A number of recent studies have used elaborate statistical models to confirm the trend, and to suggest that it is likely to continue. The most widely cited recent example is the work of Steven Pinker, and his book, *The Better Angels of Our Nature: Why Violence Has Declined*, New York: Penguin, 2012. See also his updated analysis, "Has the Decline of Violence Reversed Since the Better Angels of Our Nature Was Written?" Unpublished paper, n.d., available from *stevenpinker.com/files/pinker/files/has_the_decline_of_violence_reversed_since_the_better_angels_of_our_nature_was_written.pdf*.

4. Nadia Schadlow, "Peace and War: The Space Between," *War on the Rocks*, August 2014.

5. Lawrence Freedman has argued that Russia's tactics in Ukraine have been "driven by weakness as much as by strength." Lawrence Freedman, "Ukraine and the Art of Limited War," *War on the Rocks*, October 8, 2014.

6. Mark Galeotti, "'Hybrid War' and 'Little Green Men': How It Works and How It Doesn't," E-IR, April 16, 2015, p. 2.

7. Andràs Ràcz, *Russia's Hybrid War in Ukraine*, Report No. 43, Helsinki, Finland: The Finnish Institute of International Affairs, 2015, pp. 19-42, discusses various of the concepts at issue here — hybrid, asymmetric, nonlinear, and so on — and the distinction clearly emerges.

8. Robert Haddick, "Salami Slicing in the South China Sea," *Foreign Policy*, August 3, 2012.

9. Robert Haddick, "America Has No Answer," *War on the Rocks*, February 2014.

10. Thomas Schelling discussed this trend in *Arms and Influence*, New Haven, CT: Yale University Press, 1966, p. 27.

11. Clausewitz recognizes that war is hardly complete and distinct, that his portrait of "total war" is a partial caricature. It would be valid, he explains, if "war were a wholly isolated act" that "consisted of a single decisive act or a set of simultaneous ones" or if "the decision achieved was complete and perfect in itself."(p. 78) But none of these things is actually true. But in the real world, efforts tend "to fall short of maximum." States can't employ all their resources at once. "Warfare thus eludes the strict theoretical requirement that extremes of force be applied." Later he says war is not a "complete, untrammeled, absolute manifestation of violence" but a more qualified endeavor in which the political object determines the object and the type of force to be applied. He argues that not all wars are fought to unconditional surrender; that using political coercion to win without destroying the enemy's forces; that using "the duration of the war the bring about a gradual exhaustion of his physical and moral resistance." Carl von Clausewitz, *On War*, Michael Howard and Peter Paret, eds and trans., Princeton, NJ: Princeton University Press, 1984, p. 75.

12. The role of violence, for example, has pride of place in the trinity — a combination of chance, policy, or politics, and "primordial violence, hatred, and enmity." When he asks what means can be used to prosecute war, he answers, "There is only one: *combat*." Combat can take different forms, he admits, but quickly adds, "Everything that occurs in war results from the existence of armed forces; *but whenever armed forces, that is armed individuals,*

are used, the idea of combat must be present." Warfare therefore consists of "everything related to the fighting forces." Essentially, he says later, "war is fighting"; in a number of places, he defines it as the use of armed forces for an engagement. "War is a clash between major interests," he writes at another point, "which is resolved by bloodshed." Clausewitz, *On War*, pp. 89, 95, 127, 149. He has a whole chapter on physical danger on the battlefield, with bullets hissing past and "shot failing like hail"; cf. 113.

13. *Ibid.*, p. 87.

14. A closely related literature is that dealing with limited warfare, the various types of conflict short of the classic Clausewitzian notion of "total" war. Conflict can be limited in time, destructiveness, scope, participants, or many other ways, and so gradualist strategy could be considered one form of limited war. Freedman recently argued that "The concept of limited war . . . requires that the belligerents choose not to fight at full capacity, and so prevent a conflict gaining in intensity and expanding in both space and time.. . . . The concept comes into play only when the limits have been chosen and accepted by both parties." Freedman, "Ukraine and the Art of Limited War."

15. Sun Tzu, *The Art of War*, Samuel B. Griffith, trans. and with an introduction, London, UK: Oxford University Press, 1963, p. 73.

16. As Samuel Griffith argues in his introduction, "Never to be undertaken thoughtlessly or recklessly, war was to be preceded by measures designed to make it easy to win"; Sun Tzu, *The Art of War*, pp. 77, 79, 101; Griffith, "Introduction," in Sun Tzu, *The Art of War*, p. 39.

17. This issue's connection to current Chinese gray zone strategies is discussed in James Kraska, "How China Exploits a Loophole in International Law in Pursuit of Hegemony in East Asia," *FPRI E-Notes*, January 2015.

18. Daniel Altman, "Red Lines and Faits Accomplis," Ph.D. dissertation, Cambridge, MA: Massachusetts Institute of Technology, 2015, p. 26.

19. Steven Metz, "In Ukraine, Russia Reveals Its Mastery," *World Politics Review*, April 16, 2014.

CHAPTER 6

GRAY ZONE CAMPAIGNS IN ACTION: CHINA AND RUSSIA

This chapter seeks to illustrate the nature of gray zone strategies by examining two campaigns currently underway — China's effort to solidify its hegemony in the South China Sea, and Russia's campaign to produce dominance in Eastern Europe. The case for China and Russia's employment of gray zone strategies remains provisional. The evidence discussed is suggestive, not conclusive. It is possible that what we are seeing in both cases is an example of a disconnected series of actions rather than a coherent strategy, or else an example of something else entirely — such as a simple clandestine military *fait accompli*.

In order to evaluate whether these countries are consciously employing gray zone strategies, the analysis examines five questions:

1. Would their overall national posture and security strategies embrace such approaches?

2. Do they have identified objectives that require a shift in the rules-based order?

3. Have they developed, in official or quasi-official places, theories or concepts that support such strategies?

4. Have any official sources endorsed the idea?

5. Do we see behavior that correlates with gray zone strategies?

Even a positive answer to all five questions would not prove that a state has chosen gray zone strategies as their default approach. This section, however, argues that there is sufficient evidence in all five categories to suggest that there may be a pattern in Chinese and Russian statecraft, one that deserves further study.

Another question is whether these two actors are employing comparable strategies, or whether China and Russia are, in fact, pursuing highly distinct approaches. The analysis suggests that there are enough similarities that these two campaigns suggest the potential relevance of the gray zone concept. Yet there are significant differences between the two which once again illustrate the challenges of categorizing strategies: Russia's approach to Georgia and Ukraine is far more aggressive and militarized than anything China has yet attempted in the South China Sea. Russian approaches strain the "non-military" criteria for gray zone campaigns, and could perhaps be just as easily categorized as paramilitary invasions designed to achieve a *fait accompli*. Nonetheless, Russia's actions meet the basic definitions of gray zone strategies — most importantly, Moscow appears to view its approach as one restrained enough to avoid triggering key thresholds.

Figure 6-1 roughly plots the scope of the two campaigns on the spectrum of gray zone activities outlined in Chapter 5. In each case, the full range of activities extends to the left and right of the colored boxes — in particular, the Russian campaign encompasses the political narrative-building on the lower-intensity side of the scale. Moreover, China's use of swarming civilian maritime agencies overlaps to some degree with Russia's use of paramilitary incursions. The figure reflects the idea that, while emphasizing different places on the spectrum, both fall into the broad concept of gray zone strategies.

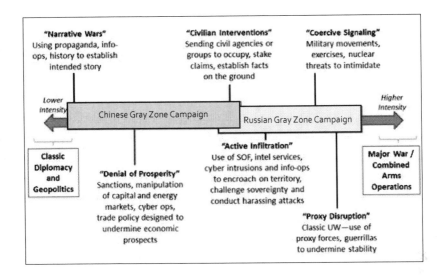

Figure 6-1. Chinese and Russian Gray Zone Strategies.

BEIJING'S GRAY ZONE STRATEGY

A leading example of such an approach has been China's pursuit of gray zone revisionism in the South China Sea. China clearly has some degree of revisionist goals, satisfying the second criteria suggested earlier. Beijing desires regional hegemony to gain control of specific resources and counterbalance, and eventually replace, U.S. geopolitical preeminence in Asia.[1] But like other measured revisionists, China's aggression is strictly bounded. It has no desire to collapse global economic institutions or create spiraling new regional instability. It has been more than willing to take patient, decades-long approaches to even vital claims in the name of preserving a global system amenable to economic growth and prosperity. It seems well aware of the advantages of recognition as a responsible global actor. For these and other reasons, China has become a measured revisionist—a state determined to change aspects of the current system without overturning it. Its basic national strategic posture would, indeed, therefore appear to call for something like gray zone strategies to pursue revisionist goals but do so while managing risk and preserving stability.[2]

There are reasons to believe that Chinese conceptions of strategy are inherently attuned to gray zone approaches. In both official and unofficial statements, Chinese strategy emphasizes the holistic, multidomain aspects of even military confrontations, tightly integrating political, diplomatic, informational, and economic elements.[3] China tends to favor patient, indirect approaches if at all possible, a preference grounded in classic Chinese strategic thought.

In recent years Chinese scholars have issued a number of theoretical works emphasizing the value of gray zone strategies. The publication of such concepts does not necessarily indicate that governments have adopted them. But a number of factors suggest that these theories are at least suggestive of state intent: They have been authored by current or former military officers; they were issued by state-run publishing sources; and there are numerous related discussions or publications or official comments that suggest these ideas have taken root and reflect at least some degree of official thinking.

The most important example of such gray zone theorizing in China is the well-known Chinese report authored by two colonels in the Chinese military entitled "Unrestricted Warfare."[4] It constitutes a vision of future conflict that breaks down the dividing lines between civilian and military affairs and between peace and war, in a persistent campaign for relative advantage. The title refers to lack of limits on use of range of tools to achieve power, not on warfare of extreme violence. "Unrestricted Warfare" contends that nonmilitary tools are becoming equally prominent and useful for the achievement of previously military objectives. Cyberattacks, financial weapons, information attacks—all of these taken together constitute the future of warfare. The "battlefield is everywhere"—the very essence of an unrestricted war.

The document is more suggestive than analytical, throwing out 100 provocations without providing solid empirical examples or operational detail. It is not as clear as it could be about the line between "unrestricted" and classic warfare, or whether the unrestricted variety is truly a substitute for major war or only an adjunct. (At times, for example, the document refers to a complex jumble of everything—long-range kinetic strikes alongside cyber operations and financial punishments.) It does not recognize as well as it could that these techniques are hardly new, and that states have dipped into the full range of the unrestricted warfare toolkit over the millennia. But it remains one of the best portraits of a different way of conceiving conflict in the gray zone.

Finally, in the Chinese case, we do appear to see behavior consonant with a state employing a gray zone strategy for revisionist intent. To achieve its goals in the South China Sea, China has taken a long series of actions that have built up a persistent claim to regional hegemony—a series of steps that would appear to add up to a coherent gray zone campaign for competitive advantage. China has employed a wide range of tools and techniques as part of this campaign.[5] It has published detailed political claims to territory within its "nine-dashed line."[6] It has generated historical narratives and documentation in support of its claims and stated a determination to resolve disputes to its satisfaction. It has deployed a "staggering variety and number of civil law enforcement and civilian commercial vessels and aircraft" in swarming and presence missions throughout the region; indeed it brought together five distinct civilian maritime agencies into a unified Coast Guard in 2013 to enhance the mutual collaboration in these forces.[7] It has employed the China National Offshore Oil Corporation for regional coercion, deploying an oil rig near the Paracel Islands in 2014. It has integrated a range of economic, diplomatic, and informational steps into a coherent campaign of influence. Figure 6-2 outlines the range of tools being employed.

Gray Zone Characteristics	China's Actions
Pursues political objectives through integrated campaigns.	• Outlined political foundations for claims in South China Sea (SCS) area. Narrative, propaganda efforts. • Numerous elements in seemingly coordinate campaign: Maritime, political, economic, military. • Theoretical foundations for integrated non-military approach.
Employs mostly non-military or non-kinetic tools.	• Paramilitary: Deployment of civilian fishing fleets and aircraft to establish presence in disputed areas, swarm and overwhelm other claimants' activities, or reinforce Chinese presence claims under pressure. • Economic: Offering direct aid or favorable trade deals, signing access agreements or joint development deals, threatening or imposing sanctions. • Energy: Use of oil rigs as presence tools; energy agreements and aid as inducements. • Diplomatic: Conducting direct coercive diplomacy, working to undermine cooperative or coalition responses to China's actions, engaging in negotiations. Establishing parallel norms and institutions that preserve basic stability of a rules-based order but shift influence to Beijing. • Informational: Formal statements, social media campaigns, publicizing narratives; use of cyber capabilities to gather and shape information, threaten punitive actions.

Figure 6-2. China's Gray Zone Campaign.

Gray Zone Characteristics	China's Actions
Strives to remain under key escalatory thresholds to avoid outright warfare.	• Seemingly clear intent to remain below thresholds of response, including UN Charter definition of "aggressive actions" that trigger self-defense provisions. • Willing to retreat to ease tensions and preserve thresholds.
Moves gradually towards its objectives rather than seeking decisive results in a short period of time.	• Long-term, incremental series of steps to achieve strategic objectives. • Willing to step backwards to ease tensions and preserve the capability for long-term progress.

Figure 6-2. China's Gray Zone Campaign. (Cont.)

Beijing has placed these tools and techniques to work supporting a long series of coercive actions. In 2012, Beijing established a settlement on Woody Island in the Paracels. In April 2012, it ratcheted up pressure on Scarborough Reef, and eventually the Philippine forces had to pull back for lack of resources. In November 2013, it declared an Air Defense Interdiction Zone (IDIZ) in the East China Sea. It has employed state-owned institutions like China National Offshore Oil Corporation to create de facto expectation of administrative control of resources, and deliberately provoked close-run military engagements with other powers in the region, especially the United States and Japan.

Taken as a whole, then, the approach would appear to meet the criteria for the pursuit of revisionist objectives by the gradual application of gray zone tools and techniques. As long ago as 2000, Andrew Scobell referred to China's emerging use of nonmilitary force in the region as a "slow-intensity conflict," a strategy of moves that tries to "lull the other claimants into believing that no conflict exists."[8] Van Jackson similarly has argued that "states that challenge the status quo are increasingly doing so in ways that are deniable, by pursuing types of coercion that make attribution difficult, or that blur the distinction between aggressor and defender." He calls this "gray-zone coercion." China, he suggests:

> has engaged in a pattern of assertiveness over territorial claims without directly employing People's Liberation Army naval forces, instead relying on non-traditional actors and non-traditional means—fishing vessels, the Coast Guard, water cannons, construction crews that build artificial islands in disputed areas, intrusive but unarmed reconnaissance drones, and 'sonic devices' that induce nausea in their targets.[9]

An important criterion distinguishing gray zone strategies from standard issue, persistent but uncoordinated great-power competition is some degree of intentionality and design. In order to have some meaningful coherence and standing, a gray zone strategy must be conceived of as an intentional campaign, with specific lines of effort and identified (even if somewhat vague) objectives. It must be deliberately chosen as an alternative to traditional military operations.

There is evidence that China's gray zone approach in the South China Sea is an intentional strategy that meets these criteria—but it is important to stress that this is a provisional judgment based on incomplete evidence. Chinese officials, for example, repeatedly have mentioned gray zone concepts. Major General Zhang Zhaozhong of China's People's Liberation Army has referred to a "cabbage strategy" for gaining influence—wrapping targeted islands with "concentric layers of Chinese fishing boats, fishing administration ships, maritime enforcements ships, and warships."[10]

China appears to coordinate various aspects of its non-military approaches to achieve holistic effect. It calibrates the degree of belligerence to keep the strategy under thresholds of response, scaling back for a year or more at a time when regional reactions becomes too intense.

At the same time, China is investing heavily in the capacity to wage major warfare. It is buying new generations of ships and aircraft, new tanks, new targeting and precision strike capabilities, and much more. It has an avowed intention to reach the frontiers of military technology and development by 2020, and to achieve various forms of military parity with the United States. Beijing clearly is not neglecting the potential for major conflict, or the value of an increasingly dominant regional military posture along traditional lines. Again, the increasing relevance of the gray zone does not imply that other forms of conflict no longer demand attention, or that they have become impossible. In fact, China's emphasis on enhanced capacity for traditional military operations is not inconsistent with a gray zone emphasis. But the gray zone is only one part of the potential spectrum of rivalry and conflict, and must be understood as such.

Gradual, gray zone strategies place the United States in an uncomfortable position. It will be more difficult to gather regional support for decisive responses to restrained seemingly nonmilitary moves by China. The gradualism of the strategy is especially problematic: China has been able to step forward boldly for a year or more with various provocative actions, then step back and wage a charm offensive to reset regional and global perceptions before another push forward. It is salami slicing its way to the achievement of its objectives, and at no point does it create a sufficient balancing dynamic to effectively check its activities. In the process, its strategy may be undermining the utility of regional strategies that assume or rely upon conclusive approaches: Elaborate plans for large-scale conflict, such as the concept of Air Sea Battle, for example, are of little use in counteracting China's gray zone gradualism.[11]

As suggested earlier, gray zone strategies come with significant costs and limitations, and these have been evident in China's campaign in the South China Sea. One source of cost is budgetary: Although precise figures are unknown, Beijing is surely paying a significant price for the maritime capabilities, day-to-day operations, and major construction projects in the region. This creates opportunity cost with other potential expenditures; abandoning the gray zone strategy, for example, might allow China to invest in additional military capabilities. Surely the more important cost, however, is geostrategic. Despite Beijing's effort to operate below various thresholds, its ambitious and aggressive gray zone posturing has provoked a significant reaction throughout the region. Other states are bolstering their maritime capabilities, coordinating their responses, and cozying up to the United States. The region increasingly views China as an imminent threat and is taking steps to balance Chinese power. In the long-run, especially if economic powerhouses like Japan and South Korea join the process, this is not a contest that China can hope to dominate.

These developments reflect one of the primary limitations to gray zone strategies, which is evident in the Chinese case. Such strategies cannot escape the basic balancing dynamic that emerges when states seek regional or global hegemony. Gray zone strategies can become counterproductive for their authors by provoking such reactions, which make the achievement of regional dominance less rather than more likely. While gray zone strategies can achieve significant short-term gains, the irony is that their reliance on long-term, patient, and gradual strategies may be misplaced. Over the long run, an accumulation of aggressive steps will provoke reactions whether or not major thresholds are crossed.

RUSSIA AND ITS PERIPHERY

A second leading example of a gray zone strategy can be found in Russia's unfolding campaign to dominate Russia's near abroad and drive wedges between U.S.-led alliances. These techniques have been in evidence not only in Ukraine over the last year or more, but also in earlier aggressive moves against Georgia and Estonia. Even Russia's energy diplomacy with Eastern Europe reflects another variant of a gray zone strategy. These actions represent something more than classic great power politics, but are designed to avoid the costs and risks of outright conflict. It is possible to view them as something more straightforward, and frankly aggressive, than gray zone strategies—a preemptive military *fait accompli* that relies heavily on conventional military forces, sometimes deployed in clandestine and deniable ways. Recent battles in Ukraine have certainly involved force-on-force firefights consistent with major combat operations, and have produced casualties numbering in the thousands. But there is significant evidence as outlined in the five categories, that Moscow consciously has undertaken gray zone approaches.[12]

As in the Chinese case and in the Russian case, we see evidence of quasi-official publications that lay a theoretical foundation for such campaigns. There is an extensive literature on nonlinear war and related issues in Russian publications. Analyst Vladislav Surkov has discussed the potential for "a future war, which involves everybody and everything, all aspects of life, while still remaining elusive in its main contours."[13] Sergei Chekanov and Sergey Bogdanov, writing about asymmetric war in 2010,[14] argued that geopolitical competition is heating up, and states will be looking for means to wage competition and conflict. The role of military force remains important, but the focus is on the indirect use of military power to achieve decisive ends in which the role of information and other nonkinetic components becomes more decisive. In a subsequent essay entitled "The Nature and Content of a New Generation War,"[15] the two authors widen their scope to include all manner of national tools that can contribute to a comprehensive campaign. Asymmetry and indirection take their ultimate forms, with states employing any mechanism available to them in order to undermine an adversary's power. The approach discards the direct, decisive mindset of conventional military operations for a more gradual and ambiguous approach that reduces costs and risks.

The defining example of such concepts, however, is an essay by Chief of the Russian General Staff Valery Gerasimov, laying out what rapidly came to be termed the "Gerasimov Doctrine" and which has also become known as "New Generation Warfare." The very first line concludes that, "In the 21st century, we have seen a tendency toward blurring the lines between the states of war and peace. Wars are no longer declared and, having begun, proceed according to an unfamiliar template." Gerasimov describes a future in which a wide range of tools can bring a society to its knees in a matter of days or weeks:

Of course, it would be easiest of all to say that the events of the "Arab Spring" are not war and so there are no lessons for us—military men—to learn. But maybe the opposite is true—that precisely these events are typical of warfare in the 21st century. In terms of the scale of the casualties and destruction, the catastrophic social, economic, and political consequences, such new-type conflicts are comparable with the consequences of any real war. The very 'rules of war' have changed. The role of nonmilitary means of achieving political and strategic goals has grown, and, in many cases, they have exceeded the power of force of weapons in their effectiveness.

Military forces merely "supplement" these activities, Gerasimov writes. "Frontal engagements of large formations of forces at the strategic and operational level are gradually becoming a thing of the past," he concludes. "Long-distance, contactless actions against the enemy are becoming the main means of achieving combat and operational goals."[16]

States using "unrestricted warfare" strategies or the approaches laid out by Gerasimov would employ a wide range of tools—economic, diplomatic, informational, military, and more. In such campaigns, outright military moves are vague or ambiguous; sometimes they are more apparent, but stop well short of large-scale conventional combined arms combat. The critical factors are the encompassing, holistic nature of the campaign and its largely nonmilitary character. The specific goals can vary, however, and need not always be as elaborate as the ones sketched out by Gerasimov. The campaigns he outlines sound more like a conventional bombing campaign conducted through other means—significant impacts through the whole range of an enemy territory to bring about the end of their regime or their surrender on some key issue. Gray zone campaigns could be used for such objectives, but they can also be employed for much more limited ends: Gaining leverage on a specific territorial dispute, for example.

Philip Karber has studied Russian tactics in Ukraine from the front lines, and argues that Moscow is using "New Generation Warfare" techniques quite explicitly, using the Ukraine campaign "to both test and perfect it." Karber's account makes clear the challenge in categorizing the Russian approach. From first-hand, front-line reporting, he describes substantial tank battles, massive artillery duels, and the movement of Russian conventional forces across the border. At one point, he uses the phrase "real war." Yet, he also defines "New Generation Warfare" in primarily nonmilitary terms: Political subversion, proxy sanctuary, "intervention" (but mostly in the form of maneuvering around the border and limited cross-border firing), coercive deterrence, and "negotiated manipulation."[17]

As in the Chinese case, Russian objectives clearly have a revisionist cast while desiring to avoid outright conflict—Russia has national interests or goals that would suggest the need for gray zone revisionism. Russian President Vladimir Putin seeks to renew Russian dominance of the near abroad, undermine the North Atlantic Treaty Organization (NATO), and reduce U.S. influence in the region. He has been trying to coerce the alignment decisions of neighboring states—Georgia and Ukraine most prominent among them—by essentially denying their right to throw their lot with the West. Yet like China, Russia's revisionism comes with strict limits. So far at least, Moscow seems anxious to preserve its standing as a responsible member of the international community.

We also see behavior that implies the existence of gray zone strategies. As Figure 6-3 suggests, the approach has drawn from a shifting array of tools.[18] These include coercive diplomacy, economic assistance, threats of energy sanctions, propaganda and information operations, cyberattacks, sponsorship of local militias and guerrilla organizations, support for pro-Moscow political movements, military maneuvers, and implied nuclear threats.[19] Further evidence of Russia's explicit adoption of gray zone strategies can be found in the significant investments in the tools and capabilities to engage in such campaigns. Moscow has built up various components of its special operating forces, Mark Galeotti notes, providing the capacity for unattributed infiltration as occurred in Ukraine. It has invested in its intelligence assets, to provide deep situational awareness for such campaigns. Moscow has expanded its propaganda tools, including the RT television channel and social media outlets.[20] All of this adds up to a significant investment in the gray zone.

Gray Zone Characteristics	Russia's Actions
Pursues political objectives through integrated campaigns.	• Outlined political objections to NATO/Western policies in Eastern Europe, basis for Russian claims of hegemony, territorial claims. Narrative, propaganda efforts. • Numerous elements in a seemingly coordinated campaign: Propaganda, political subversion, unconventional warfare, cyber, economic, military. • Uses negotiation process as a cover for campaign. Generates enemy "violations" of ceasefires and negotiated agreements to justify actions.

Figure 6-3. Russia's Gray Zone Campaign.

| Employs mostly non-military or non-kinetic tools. | • Paramilitary: Use proxy forces, from paid demonstrators to friendly militias to plain-clothes special forces, to infiltrate, cause disruption, eventually seize elements of state authority in targeted areas. Create proxy sanctuaries to protect allied forces; control transportation nodes in targeted areas. "Rebrand" own forces, even high-end motorized forces, as local proxies. At high end use direct military fires to support local proxies: Artillery, direct action in extreme cases.
• Political: Identify socio-political vulnerabilities in target states, especially ethnonational diasporas. Support separatist movements. Bribe local political leaders and media figures; manipulation of targeted and coordinated corruption.
• Economic: Sanctions or threat of same, targeted financial punishments, withdrawal of capital; generating a crisis to spark capital flight and collapse of FDI.
• Energy: Use of energy dependencies for coercive effect.
• Diplomatic: General proposals and negotiating positions that support narrative and objectives; reach out to friendly states, dampen opposition.
• Informational: Formal statements, social media campaigns, publicizing narratives; employ friendly NGOs in target state to parrot narrative.
• Cyber: Use of cyber capabilities to gather and shape information, threaten punitive actions. |
| Strives to remain under key escalatory thresholds to avoid outright warfare. | • Strategy avoids directly challenging areas of U.S./Western vital national interests: Crimea vs. Kiev. |

Figure 6-3. Russia's Gray Zone Campaign. (Cont.)

Matthew Kroenig has described this strategy as "a combination of hybrid warfare and nuclear brinkmanship." The goal is to use various levels of force "to make gradual territorial revisions against nearby NATO members." Moscow wants to avoid an outright conventional clash with NATO, and so it uses "hybrid warfare to make its revisionist actions as subtle as possible, avoiding moves that would trigger an automatic, robust response." It employs tactics such as claiming to rescue Russian nationals, cyberwar, propaganda, clandestine special operations forces operations especially targeted against government facilities, economic sanctions, massing of coercive regular military forces at the border, all "to make small but meaningful gains short of outright invasion."[21] In NATO responses, official as well as unofficial, the term "hybrid warfare" has been widely used to describe these activities — though as we have seen what these analyses really have in mind is something closer to the concept of gray zone conflict.[22]

As Moscow's strategy has played out, the limits and costs of its aggressive gray zone strategy have become more evident. Lawrence Freedman has pointed out, for example, that the celebrated militias and fifth-columnists sponsored by Moscow have run into significant operational difficulties. The somewhat random collection of units and forces drawn together for the campaign were difficult to coordinate, and some resisted direction from Russia. It was all well and good to suggest destabilizing a neighbor, but once the campaign shifted to the traditional sphere, Moscow had to consider the challenge of occupying parts of a hostile state. Its efforts to generate false narratives, Freedman reminds us, achieved little in the West, where its aggression was seen for what it was.[23]

Russia has paid a tremendous price for its gray zone adventurism — economic sanctions, political alienation, and military countermoves. The United States and a number of NATO allies have been training Ukrainian units, and learning much about Russian operational art in the process — lessons that could be put to good use if the conflict were ever to escalate. Joshua Rovner has ably catalogued the results of Putin's gambits:

> In the last 2 years, he has all but ruined his aspiration to return Russia to the ranks of the great powers.

His ham-fisted annexation of Crimea, along with his transparent support for secessionists in the ongoing civil war in East Ukraine, has been disastrous for Russian interests. Putin's adventurism led to stock market chaos, a major currency crisis, and staggering levels of capital flight—all of which have compounded the problem of collapsing oil prices. The loss of revenue is damaging Russia's conventional military power because the government will struggle mightily to modernize its forces. Meanwhile, Putin has breathed new life into NATO, an alliance that had been searching for common purpose and sagging under the weight of the war in Afghanistan.[24]

At the same time, the ongoing conflict has become a festering drain on resources and national will. If Moscow's aim in the use of gray zone tactics was to avoid significant retaliation, it has failed miserably.

CONCLUSION

There would appear to be sufficient evidence to suggest, therefore, that both China and Russia have explicitly chosen gray zone-style strategies to pursue their measured revisionist goals. As noted earlier, this claim remains provisional; the evidence is suggestive but not conclusive. Nonetheless, there is enough to suggest that the United States and its friends and allies ought to do more to understand the nature of gray zone conflict. Chapter 7 offers a number of provisional hypotheses about such conflicts.

ENDNOTES - CHAPTER 6

1. See, for example, Nayan Chanda, "China's Long-Range Salami Tactics in East Asia," *Huffington Post,* January 27, 2014; and John Chen, "Get Comfortable Being Uncomfortable: Uncertain-

ty, Brinksmanship, and Salami-Slicing in East Asia," *Georgetown Security Studies Review*, February 1, 2015.

2. Debate continues, of course, over just how limited its aspirations are, or will remain. Jonathan Holslag has argued that, to fulfill them, "China must become the most powerful country in Asia by far, and attain the power to deter other protagonists by force." He lays out four specific goals of Chinese foreign policy: Control of key frontier lands like Tibet; sustain Party rule through economic growth and stability; win respect for Chinese sovereignty; and to "recover so-called 'lost territory,'" from Taiwan to South China Sea islands to areas of the East China Sea and areas of the Himalayas contested with India. Jonathan Holslag, "The Smart Revisionist," p. 96.

3. Timothy L. Thomas, "China's Conception of Military Strategy," *Parameters*, Vol. 44, No. 4, Winter 2014-15, pp. 41-42.

4. Qiao Liang and Wang Xiangsui, *Unrestricted Warfare*, Beijing, China: PLA Literature and Arts Publishing House, 1999.

5. An excellent source of data on the range of Chinese gray zone activities is Christopher Yung and Patrick McNulty, "China's Tailored Coercion," Report 5, Maritime Strategy Series, Washington, DC: Center for a New American Security, January 26, 2015.

6. Mohan Malik, "Historical Fiction: China's South China Sea Claims," *World Affairs*, May-June, 2013, available from *www. worldaffairsjournal.org/article/historical-fiction-china%E2%80%99s-south-china-sea-claims*.

7. James Kraska, "How China Exploits a Loophole in International Law in Pursuit of Hegemony in East Asia," FPRI E-Notes, January 2015.

8. Andrew Scobell, "Slow-Intensity Conflict in the South China Sea," *E-Notes*, Philadelphia, PA: Foreign Policy Research Institute, August 2000. "China's actions," Robert Haddick — one of the keenest observers of gradualist strategies — has written:

> look like an attempt to gradually and systematically establish legitimacy for its claims in the region. It has stood up a local

civilian government, which will command a permanent military garrison. It is asserting its economic claims by leasing oil and fishing blocks inside other countries' EEZs, and is sending its navy to thwart development approved by other countries in the area.

See Robert Haddick, "Salami Slicing in the South China Sea," *Foreign Policy*, August 3, 2012.

9. Van Jackson, Testimony before the House Committee on Foreign Affairs, Subcommittee on Asia and the Pacific, Washington, DC, February 26, 2015, pp. 1-3.

10. Robert Haddick, "America Has No Answer," War on the Rocks, February 2014.

11. Zachary Keck, "Shaming Won't Stop China's Salami-Slicing," *The Diplomat*, July 16, 2014.

12. See Will Cathcart and Joseph Epstein, "Why Putin's Phony Wars Work Better than 'Real' Ones," *The Daily Beast*, August 8, 2015. Molly McKew and Gregory Maniatis argue that Russia has developed a version of "pop-up war — nimble and covert — that is likely to be the design of the future." See "Playing By Putin's Tactics," *Washington Post*, March 9, 2014, available from *https://www.washingtonpost.com/opinions/playing-by-putins-tactics/2014/03/09/b5233b90-a558-11e3-a5fa-55f0c77bf39c_story.html*.

13. See the discussion in Andràs Ràcz, *Russia's Hybrid War in Ukraine*, Report No. 43, Helsinki, Finland: The Finnish Institute of International Affairs, 2015, pp. 34-42.

14. S. G. Chekinov and S. A. Bogdanov, "Asymmetrical Actions to Maintain Russia's Military Security," *Military Thought*, No. 1, 2010, available from *www.eastviewpress.com/Files/MT_FROM%20THE%20CURRENT%20ISSUE_No.1_2010_small.pdf*.

15. S. G. Chekinov and S. A. Bogdanov, "The Nature and Content of a New Generation War," *Military Thought*, October-December 2013, available from *www.eastviewpress.com/Files/MT_FROM%20THE%20CURRENT%20ISSUE_No.4_2013.pdf*.

16. Valery Gerasimov, "The Value of Science in Prediction," *Military-Industrial Courier*, February 27, 2013, trans. in "The Gersimov Doctrine and Russian Non-Linear War," *Moscow's Shadows*, available from *https://inmoscowsshadows.wordpress.com/2014/07/06/the-gerasimov-doctrine-and-russian-non-linear-war/*.

17. Dr. Phillip A. Karber, "'Lessons Learned' from the Russo-Ukrainian War: Personal Observations," Alexandria, VA: The Potomac Foundation, July 6, 2015.

18. Examples in the figure are drawn in part from Ràcz, *Russia's Hybrid War in Ukraine*, pp. 57-70.

19. Steven Metz describes the resulting strategy this way: "Moscow's complex, multidimensional offensive uses intimidation, misinformation and any organization or group that can serve its interests." Specific actions include disinformation campaigns, economic pressure, military coercion, the use of quasi-military groups and militias. "Moscow has adopted, even mastered, a form of unrestricted warfare optimized for the age of pervasive information, economic connectivity and social media," Steven Metz, "In Ukraine, Russia Reveals Its Mastery of Unrestricted Warfare," *World Politics Review*, April 16, 2014.

20. Mark Galeotti, "'Hybrid War' and 'Little Green Men': How It Works and How It Doesn't," E-IR, April 16, 2015, p. 2.

21. Matthew Kroenig, "Facing Reality: Getting NATO Ready for a New Cold War," *Survival*, Vol. 57, No. 1, February-March 2015, pp. 53-54. See also Lawrence Freedman, "Ukraine and the Art of Crisis Management," *Survival*, Vol. 56, No. 3, June-July 2014, p. 9. See also A. Wess Mitchell and Jakob Grygiel, "'Salami-Slicing' and Deterrence," *The American Interest*, November 18, 2014.

22. Agence-France Presse, "NATO Allies Brace for Russia's Hybrid Warfare," *Defense News*, March 18, 2015, available from *www.defensenews.com/story/defense/international/europe/2015/03/18/nato-allies-brace-for-russias-hybrid-warfare/24979545/*.

23. Lawrence Freedman, "Ukraine and the Art of Limited War," *Survival*, Vol. 56, No. 6, December 2014-January 2015, pp. 15-18, 23-24, 26.

CHAPTER 7

SEVEN HYPOTHESES ON THE GRAY ZONE

In order to understand the essence of the challenge posed by gray zone conflict, this chapter offers seven propositions on the character of this tool. These are offered as hypotheses rather than conclusions because they remain provisional and suggestive. They represent invitations to delve further into theoretical and empirical analysis to determine the real challenge posed by such modes of statecraft.

HYPOTHESIS ONE: GRAY ZONE CAMPAIGNS WILL CONSTITUTE THE DEFAULT MODE OF CONFLICT IN COMING DECADES

This hypothesis flows logically from the portrait of the emerging shape of world politics developed in the first few chapters of this monograph. If world politics are indeed likely to be characterized by a growing number of "measured revisionists"; if these measured revisionists (and others) will be able to rely on gradual, incremental approaches to achieving their interests and goals; and if they have at their disposal a growing array of nontraditional tools other than classic military force to conduct those efforts, then gray zone strategies stand to become the default means of global competition. The potential for traditional major conflict will remain ever-present, but largely as a result of misperception, miscommunication or accident rather than as the purposeful strategy of a major power.

There is strong reason to believe that the coming decades are likely to witness growing tension and rivalry in international politics. This is a function of the growing proportion of revisionism within the preferences and desires of major powers. But it may also stem from the more general multipolarity of the emerging system, in which a larger number of rising powers, whether truly revisionist or not, will be jostle for influence and power. At the same time, continued economic challenges and other factors are helping to fuel aggressive ethno-nationalism in many emerging countries, exacerbating the underlying sense of grievance, suspicion and rivalry in the system.

The upshot of such trends is that we can expect the next 2-plus decades to be a time of burgeoning competition. But it will also be a time when most states recognize that their vital interests, including national prosperity and the security of the governing regimes, rely to a significant degree on the economic, diplomatic, and military benefits of participation in some version of a rules-based order. The emerging pattern, already well in evidence, would seem to be a sort of constrained or measured rivalry, and gray zone strategies represent a leading adaptation to such a context. "Every age had its own kind of war," Clausewitz argued[1]—and in the coming decades, the sort of warfare, or conflict, most appropriate to the context could be one that allows major powers to compete short of the threshold of major war.

As suggested earlier, though, this hypothesis does not imply that major war has become "impossible." The evidence supports a proposition that the **conscious choices of responsible state leadership** would seldom, if ever, find reason to engage in large-scale conflict, and would prefer to operate in the gray zone. But wars can also arise through unplanned escalation, miscalculation, and accident. China, Russia, India, and other states are investing heavily in traditional military capabilities. U.S. national security strategy cannot proceed as if war is out of the question — only that, when dealing with the intentional strategies of leading powers, it will generally be dealing with gray zone approaches.

If valid, this hypothesis would have significant implications. It suggests that the most common national security threats will stem from gray zone initiatives rather than traditional military aggression. It implies that states are likely to invest more resources in the tools that make gray zone campaigns possible, everything from elite direct action special operations forces to social media capabilities and civilian coast guards. It also suggests that greater emphasis and resources should be devoted to developing concepts and doctrines tailored for gray zone environments.

HYPOTHESIS TWO: GRAY ZONE STRATEGIES DEMAND A NEW THEORY OF CONFLICT

In the process, gray zone campaigns would also seem to call for a new theory of conflict — a set of principles and theories of success in gray zone environments. As we are already seeing, the authors of gray zone approaches hope to place defenders in challenging positions strewn with dilemmas. Responding in traditional ways might not work, and can even be counterproductive. Gray zone conflict must be understood in fundamentally different ways from major warfare.

In major war, for example, classic doctrine holds that success comes from focus, concentration, speed, and decisiveness. The principles of gray zone conflict will be very different. Sample operational principles for success in the gray zone might include:

- *The ultimate objectives of any campaign will derive from political interests and goals that will be entirely contingent to the situation.* The essential purpose of any gray zone campaign is to create new political facts on the ground consonant with the aggressing state's interests. This principle is similar to Carl von Clausewitz's classic dictum that war serves political objectives, but in a much more encompassing manner: Every battlefield tactic must be conceived in political terms.

- *Success depends on remaining below key thresholds* that would bring the conflict into a different realm. Patience is more important than rushing, if the risk is triggering a massively disproportionate reaction. As Russia discovered when moving on from Crimea to Ukraine proper, the cardinal sin in gray zone campaigns is becoming too ambitious. Once a campaign has triggered a disproportionate response, the advantage of the gray zone realm has been lost, and the risks of escalation grow.

- *Efforts must be coordinated to achieve effects greater than the sum of their parts.* Success in gray zone campaigns is all about holistic effects. Again, this is similar to concepts of combined arms and joint operations, but, like the issue of politics, it extends the insight to its natural conclusion. It points to further development of cross-boundary, interagency collaboration on gray zone campaigns, a goal that remains elusive within the U.S. Government.

- *Defense leaders must rethink what is considered the core or basic effort and what is considered an option or branch.* Today, military planning focuses on the moment when conventional operations begin—Phase III, in the current parlance. It is the hub around which all efforts revolve. Other places on the spectrum (either pre-war or post-war) are considered supporting branches of the main effort. Increasingly in a gray zone world, however, U.S. planners will need to take Phase 0 and Phase 1 activities seriously as the core effort, with a large-scale Phase III operation only emerging as a potential option if the gray zone crisis escalates. This reinforces the lesson that gray zone conflicts blur the boundaries between military and civilian endeavors: Military operational planning will likely be forced to give much greater attention to activities and phases traditionally discounted, or left to civilian agencies.

- *In most cases, everything will depend on an effective narrative that becomes broadly accepted*, at least within target populations (which can be a subset of a state). In classic military operations, unconditional victories can be won by states with bankrupt narratives. This will seldom be the case in the gray zone.

- *Gray zone campaigns will demand more ongoing adaptation and experimentation.* Planning for conventional military operations is designed to produce an effective force at the outset of a war capable of winning the conflict in relatively short order, using the concepts, doctrines, and capabilities in place from the start. Adaptation and innovation take place during every war, of course. But in gray zone campaigns, the balance between pre-existing approaches and adapted ones may change significantly. Because of the wide range of tools engaged in the conflict, the different forms and intensities it can take, and the groping, ambiguous nature of gradual approaches, these campaigns will likely demand a much higher degree of experimentation and learning-by-doing. They will call for a greater emphasis on innovation (both in concepts and capabilities), rapid prototyping, and flexibility in the basic strategy being employed.

- In gray zone contests, *success or failure will usually be a function of the relative social resilience and vulnerabilities of the two sides.* Rivals in gray zone conflict will depend most of all on larger strengths, weaknesses, and realities more than the quality of the tools employed. As an example, when states have weaknesses in their political unity, rivals can use that as the foundation to construct aggressive narratives and destabilize the state.

As noted earlier, U.S. military operational doctrine tends to focus on the major combat operations phase of a conflict. U.S. Joint Operational Planning approaches and procedures are all about getting to "Phase III" so that the United States can "win" in traditional terms. Yet, a major purpose of gray zone strategies is to ensure that, by the time Phase III kicks off, the enemy has already lost. Their political situation, social cohesion, ability to rally international support, logistical base, battlefield awareness, and many other critical sources of strength will be to atrophied that they will either surrender to the gray zone aggressor's political goals short of major combat, or else collapse quickly when it begins. In addition to studying the broad principles of conflict in the gray zone as suggested earlier, therefore, the U.S. Government should develop operational doctrines for these other phases of conflict.

HYPOTHESIS THREE: GRAY ZONE CAMPAIGNS GENERATE A SENSE OF PERSISTENT WARFARE

By making it more difficult to recognize the difference between peace and war, gray zone strategies are likely to foster a sense of relentless confrontation and invite the perception in the capitals of major powers that they are already at war with rivals or competitors. This is increasingly the flavor, for example, of the U.S. official dialogue on China, and becoming so of Russia as well.

National leaders expect classic geopolitical competition, even among friends and, in some cases, allies. States spy on one another, seek relative advantage in trade deals, use cyber techniques to gather information (sometimes to benefit their domestic industries), engage in industrial policy, and employ tariffs and nontariff barriers to boost their economy, and much more. In other words, they play at the "low intensity" end of the gray zone conflict spectrum on a regular basis, without creating a sense of bellicose confrontation.

By moving the scale of competition toward the right side of the spectrum, however, gray zone strategies risk replacing a sense of generally accepted levels of competition with a bitter and mutually hostile environment. Spying and seeking economic advantage is one thing; dispatching civilian fleets or covert infiltration units to generate persistent coercive pressure is a very different proposition. Many countries in Eastern Europe surely feel that Russia is at war with them today, and many U.S. national security officials believe the same about China. What this means is unclear, but that is part of the character—and risk—of gray zone approaches: Exactly what constitutes being "at war" becomes something in the eye of the beholder. A continuous series of aggressive actions built around elaborate political claims will come to be seen as a war-like campaign. State interpretations of others' goals and intentions may harden as all sides begin to view gray zone activities as evidence of limitless revisionism.

Such a perception would lay the groundwork for spirals of hostility, arms races, and other unstable outcomes. It might make it easier for states to make escalation decisions, since the perception will not be that they are starting a war—only taking the next logical step in one. Such heightened sense of conflict will also make it less likely that competitive states would be able to cooperate in areas where they genuinely share mutual interests.

As noted in Chapter 5, washing away the line between peacetime and wartime will create significant legal dilemmas for U.S. policy—a process that has been well underway over the past 15 years. Both U.S. and international law make important distinctions between what is allowed in peace as opposed to wartime. The United States has stretched that distinction during its war on terror, unilaterally determining itself to be at war in ways that the international community has not always accepted. If the pattern becomes truly generalized—if gray zone campaigns make the difference between peace and war almost moot—then important legal restraints on state action could be lost.

HYPOTHESIS FOUR: GRAY ZONE CONFLICT INCREASES THE POTENTIAL FOR INADVERTENT WAR

In one sense, the greater reliance on gray zone strategies could be a hopeful trend in international security: States adopting gray zone approaches have chosen to avoid major war. In fact, these strategies create a whole range of risks all their own. Given the constraints suggested earlier, the most likely routes to war are through misperception, accident, or miscalculation. Gradualist strategies set the stage for all three.

States may feel the ability to take greater risks with gray zone tools, for example, convinced of their ability to restrain escalation, only to find that specific actions, or the sum of several gray zone tools, begins to push the conflict up the escalatory ladder. Once a gray zone campaign is underway, moreover, it is easy to imagine the collection of actions creating a siege mentality on the part of the defender, leading to progressively more violent forms of confrontation. Aggressors may underestimate a defender's willingness to hit back and perhaps escalate in order to deter future meddling, thus sparking a spiral of conflict.[2]

In these and other ways, gray zone strategies are invitations to misperception. When Thomas Schelling discusses "the power to bind oneself," he is looking for strength in deterrent or reassuring promises by making the realm of potential choice very limited in a crisis. In a famous line, Schelling argued that "It is essential, therefore, for maximum credibility, to leave as little room as possible for judgment or discretion in carrying out the threat."[3] The emphasis is on threats that are credible, with specific, stated, or clearly implied objectives. Gray zone strategies are by definition ambiguous, with their goals and techniques masked and often explicitly denied. What the author of the strategies actually wants may not be clear—even to them. They often leave equivocal the commitments in play and, to some extent, even the national interests involved.

Schelling's discussion of the manipulation of risk also highlights the dangers. In a bargaining situation, either or both (or all) sides may use the risk of escalation as a coercive tool. It is the use of unpredictable actions to create danger that makes countries want to give in and step back from the brink. The question, he argues, is usually not between "peace" and "war"—it is whether one or both sides are willing to take some risk with an undefined danger of war. "It is the essence of a crisis that the participants are not fully in control of events," he explains. Their mutual awareness of this fact contributes to the coercive power of risk-taking. He specifically highlights limited war as not merely a direct means to an end, but also an "action that enhances the risk of a greater war" and thus a form of risk-taking coercion.[4]

The danger here, of course, is that misinterpreted lessons from a contest of risk-taking could spiral into wider conflict. There is a real risk, Schelling explains, that "the other will genuinely misinterpret how far he is invited to go. If one side yields on a series of issues, when the matters at stake are not critical, it may be difficult to communicate to the other just when a vital issue has been reached."[5] This is precisely the danger with gray zone strategies. If Russia can take 150 smallish steps toward the destabilization of Ukraine, it will be exceedingly difficult to convey that the 151st might cross some invisible threshold. The problem can also become more fundamental: Britain and France had acceded to dozens of German provocations in the years leading to 1939, and, by the time the Wehrmacht massed to invade Poland, London and Paris's insistence that they would respond this time fell on deaf ears. Gray zone strategies can create an **inherent** and inevitable lack of clarity on red lines that invites escalation and undermines deterrence.

Having been allowed to get away with many gradual steps, a gray zone aggressor's appetite may be whetted. If progress bogs down, it may be more likely to escalate than if never allowed to begin at all. This may be part of the story with regard to Russia's actions in Ukraine, which flowed from a burst of confidence in the wake of the astonishingly successful seizure of Crimea.

Viewed from the other side of the dispute, though, the opposite dynamic can be equally dangerous: Having taken dozens of steps forward, a gray zone aggressor may walk itself into a perception of emergent interests, and willingness to take further risk, that it did not have to begin with. In the gray zone strategist's own mind, the accumulation of small steps may create, over time, what is to them a hard-and-fast commitment—one that is missed by a potential challenger engaging in wishful thinking. (The incremental U.S. commitment to the Vietnam War is one example of how individual choices can accumulate to the point where credibility is at stake.) Even if a challenger begins a process, assuming that they intend to remain within the gray zone, the very aspect of such strategies that creates a dilemma for the defender—the fact that, on its own, each step does not engage vital interests—can lull the aggressor into taking so many actions that they **generate** a situation of vital interests for themselves. Once Russia has taken 100 gray zone actions toward Ukraine, for example, including the publication of extensive political narratives justifying its claims, it may have backed itself into a corner from which it cannot withdraw. If the gray zone strategy cannot generate success for its political objectives, it may feel compelled to escalate.

Part of the danger stems from the fact that the authors of gray zone strategies do not see themselves as aggressors. They believe that they are **responding** to American and allied provocations. This self-perception creates a real risk is of a cycle of mutually-escalating gradualist actions.

Eventually, the aggressor, if its campaign continues to expand, is likely to trip over some sort of an escalatory threshold. The problem is that, in gray zone campaigns even more so than traditional military confrontations, neither side has a very good sense of where precisely these thresholds are. If the victim of the gradualist moves believes it has no good response and risks being salami sliced to death, it may decide it has no alternative but to escalate—and it might do so fairly randomly, at a moment or on an issue that the aggressor has no way to anticipate. It may be impossible to know in advance when the defender will reach their point of intolerance, because the judgment is as much subjective, political, and personality-driven as it is rational and objective. Eventually, "someone is likely to draw a red line somewhere," Robert Haddick has argued:

> The issue for U.S. officials is whether they will be the ones to do that drawing, and thus retain the initiative, or whether someone else, having lost confidence in Washington, will do it instead. When that happens, the U.S. will find itself reacting to events, rather than shaping a favorable outcome in advance.[6]

The risk of escalation is magnified by the widespread use of proxies in gray zone strategies. Because such campaigns often involve an integrated but not fully coordinated network of paramilitary forces, civilian government agencies, hackers, propagandists, allies and outright mercenaries, the initiator of gray zone campaigns will seldom have full control over the outcome. The natural tendencies toward friction in conflict are magnified when the opposing forces are not largely cohesive armies but somewhat arbitrary grab-bags of actors, some of whom have little stake in stability. The potential for state-sponsored but self-directed organizations to generate escalatory spirals is very real.

From a geopolitical standpoint, gray zone tactics also risk escalation in part by complicating the task of interpreting the intentions of rising powers. International relations literature has noted the challenges of uncertainty in world politics, and specifically the difficulty of being sure about the intentions of others. This is, in fact, the leading engine of instability in neorealism and, to some degree, in many other classic and recent variants of realist thought. It is precisely because states cannot be certain about what others intend that they feel the need to prepare for the worst, and generate security dilemmas.[7] Such tactics also blur the lines between status quo and revisionist powers. They can allow a state to masquerade as a status quo power while working energetically on a revisionist agenda.

Gray zone strategies target a weak spot of the self-enforcing aspect of the international system. A critical norm is the unwillingness of most states to risk exclusion from the overall system with acts of such obvious violence and aggression that they become outcasts. Interests dictate otherwise. But the precise vulnerability of the international system is the thinness of its regulatory architecture: Whereas on the domestic front, a "gradualist" approach to overthrowing one's neighbor might quickly run afoul of the dense network of laws and regulations governing interactions of citizens (running afoul, for example, of harassment or trespassing laws or building codes), on the international scene the legal network is far less well-established. Adventurists can get away with a lot more before they hit the tripwire of the self-enforced cooperative security that reflects shared interests. Put into the language of international relations theory, it is more difficult for classic balancing dynamics to operate when members of the system cannot decide whether a state needs to be balanced at all.

One reason states hesitate to take the revisionist route is that revisionism generates reactions and can be self-defeating. Gray zone strategies, in effect, split the difference, and make it difficult for anyone—even officials in the aggressive state itself—to know if its agenda is truly revisionist or not. Incremental moves adopted as part of a gray zone strategy create a sort of ongoing game in which each side must decide whether to continue to play—to take more moves, to escalate, or step back. If the established power believes that the challengers have limited aims, the best course is to appease; if they are a new Hitler, with boundless goals, the established power should stand fast. Such uncertainty over the challenger's real intentions confront the established power with a large and ongoing dilemma: "The earlier the declining state draws the line, the stronger it is, and the higher its expected payoff in the event of war. But the earlier it draws the line, the higher the probability of an unnecessary war."[8]

HYPOTHESIS FIVE: GRAY ZONE CAMPAIGNS UNDERMINE DETERRENCE

Over time, a major risk of gray zone campaigns is that they could dissolve the credibility of U.S. commitments and deterrent threats. Indeed, this is, to some degree, the conscious intent of the authors of such strategies. Beyond the progress achieved toward political goals, with each small step that goes unpunished and unreversed, a revisionist lays more seeds of doubt that the United States (or others) would respond to something bigger.[9]

This effect can occur because gray zone campaigns disrupt the basic action-reaction dynamic of game theoretic approaches to rivalry and deterrence. The assumption of such theories is that two (or more) sides interact through relatively clear signals of their interests and intent, and that both sides are playing on a chessboard where interests and risks are objectively available. Russia knows, for example, that the Baltic states are North Atlantic Treaty Organization (NATO) members and understands the U.S. commitment to Article V of the Alliance; NATO can further signal intent via a number of actions. In theoretical terms, a good example of available preferences as a guide to interactive choice is the prisoner's dilemma: The assumed players can see the lineup of rewards.

Gray zone strategies complicate this process and raise ambiguities at many levels of signaling and deterrence. Just what intent may be at stake is not always clear, because there can be a wide gulf between the importance of one step in a gradualist chain and the ultimate effect of the whole series. States intentionally conceal their intentions in gray zone campaigns, meaning that it is difficult, if not impossible, to reliably read the goals of other actors into the situation. In short, gray zone strategies interrupt the process of accurately conveying intentions, making strategic interactions far more fluid and ambiguous.

At the same time, by generating a long series of actions that do not very often spark effective countermoves, gray zone strategies can undermine deterrence more directly, by ruining the confidence that the defender will act. As two scholars have argued:

> The second way deterrence can fail is gradual, through a chipping-away at the credibility of the leading power in the system. . . . [O]ne of the parties is intentionally seeking to readjust the *status quo* undergirded by deterrence by means of a gradual alteration of expectations and credibility. The revisionist side wants to engender a gradual failure of deterrence because it considers the existing geopolitical order not to be attuned to its interests or prestige. . . . The objective is to alter in a steady and almost stealthy way the expectations of future behavior that keep deterrence alive. That is, the revisionist power wants to make all parties involved — the rival as well as his allies — believe present promises of behavior will not be honored in the future. Once such a belief sets in, the options for the targeted powers are limited to accepting the new geopolitical reality or restoring the *status quo ante*. In either case, deterrence has failed — not violently, but in the realm of perceptions and expectations.[10]

Thomas Schelling's classic discussion of signaling and credibility emphasized the danger that small violations of deterrent threats could snowball. The reason why the United States had to defend California, he argued — apart from its intrinsic value — was that the United States could not surrender California and sustain its pledge to defend Oregon or Florida. "Once they [the aggressors] cross a line into a new class of aggression," he argued, "into a set of areas or assets that we always claimed we would protect, we may even deceive *them* if we do not react vigorously."[11] Yet gray zone strategies can create precisely such a situation, in which the aggressor is allowed to "cross lines into new classes of aggression" because the campaign is so cleverly designed that no single step provides an opportunity to "react vigorously."

The danger, then, is not merely to a specific deterrent pledge or bilateral relationship—it is to the structure of the rules-based order in general, and the credibility of U.S. and allied power that underpins that order. We can see the first hints of this in Eastern Europe today, for example, with the widely-held perception that Russia has been able to wage a version of war against neighboring states without being decisively confronted. This perception is exaggerated—as we have seen, Russia has paid a significant price for its gray zone adventurism. But to the degree that other potential aggressors **believe** that it has succeeded, the credibility of U.S. deterrent threats in other theaters, especially in relation to gray zone aggression, will decline.

A particular challenge in terms of the effects of gray zone aggression on credibility is that the United States will not recognize the threat for what it is until too late. If Iran were to launch a war of aggression in the Persian Gulf, the implications of a failure to respond would be obvious. (Indeed, the risks of such failures can be much more obvious once aggression has occurred rather than beforehand—a phenomenon we see in the Korean War and other cases.) The costs of not responding for the future of U.S. credibility will be fairly obvious. But if Iran takes 50 gradual gray zone actions to undermine its neighbors, the dangers to U.S. credibility of any one action — or any five or 10 — will be masked. This will continue until the actions reach some critical mass, at which point the injury to the reliability of U.S. promises might be irrecoverable.

HYPOTHESIS SIX: GRAY ZONE CONFLICT DEPENDS UPON LARGER SOCIAL, POLITICAL AND ECONOMIC FACTORS FOR SUCCESS OR FAILURE

The idea that war serves political objectives is hardly new. But while the operations of major combat serve political ends and are meaningless absent some higher political goal, the day-to-day operations of traditional military campaigns are themselves somewhat independent of the political sphere. The success or failure of the Union Army at Gettysburg, PA, had huge political ramifications, but success or failure on that battlefield had everything to do with military operational decisions that were isolated from the larger context.

In gray zone conflict, there is no such segmentation. The outcomes of gray zone conflicts will seldom be determined by the operations or campaigns themselves — they will be the product of larger forces. Russia's success (or failure) in its various campaigns has been a product of local social and political factors more than the skill or resources involved in its own operations. Indeed, gray zone techniques can properly be thought of tools to take advantage of pre-existing political, social, or economic vulnerabilities rather than as efforts capable of achieving decisive results on their own.

Mark Galeotti refers to the failure of Russia to undermine Ukraine as a whole and suggests that "the military is purely part of a political campaign, and that has been a disastrous failure." Authors of gray zone campaigns, he urges, must keep in mind that success "depends above all on a clear and accurate understanding of the political context in which it will operate." The whole point of gray zone campaigns is that their "diverse components must be effectively combined to win the underlying 'political war' to achieve the desired aim."[12] The openness of the current Russian economy makes Moscow vulnerable to being alienated from global trading and capital markets. It cannot prolong an endless gray zone campaign is the result is that Russia is alienated from the world economy.

From the standpoint of defending against these strategies, Phillip Karber emphasizes the importance of denying gray zone aggressors the social and political leverage points they use to fracture the stability of their targets. In Eastern Europe, for example, he stresses the importance of providing ethnic Russian minorities with a strong stake in the societies, and eliminating the official corruption on which gray zone infiltration tactics can feed.[13]

A powerful example of these lessons can be drawn from the Cold War. The Soviet Union threw every manner of gray zone weapon at the West in the form of its active measures, and none did serious damage. This was not due to the lack of sophistication of those campaigns, or the resources or commitment invested in them. It was a product, quite simply, of the ultimate truth of the Cold War: The Western socioeconomic system was stronger, and long-term trends favored the West. Mutual gray zone harassment was destined to have a much greater effect on the Soviet Union because of the inherent vulnerabilities of its system and the relative robustness of liberal democracy. Responding to gray zone campaigns is all about enhancing the political resilience of the target state.

This was George Kennan's greatest insight. The West would win the Cold War, he believed, because of its social and economic, not military, superiority. The goal of its military and geostrategic efforts was merely to avoid defeat, keep the Communist world from gaining a false sense of momentum through conquest, and wait for history's persistent energies to do their work. Our task is much the same with gray zone strategies today.

As suggested earlier, gray zone tactics are often the strategy of the weak, not the strong. They allow states like Russia and Iran—otherwise being bowled over by the tide of history—to find avenues to exercise power and pursue their regional ambitions. The key for the United States, then, is not so much to become the world master of gray zone tactics on the small scale. It is to attend to the big picture and ensure that larger trends work to the U.S. advantage.

HYPOTHESIS SEVEN: GRAY ZONE CAMPAIGNS HAVE POWERFUL LIMITATIONS

Some of the recent literature on gray zone techniques has an urgent or even defeatist tone, implying that these techniques provide huge advantages to revisionists determined to undermine U.S. power and gain relative advantage. This analysis has conveyed some of the opportunities reflected in such strategies. But, as I argued earlier, it is also important to appreciate their limitations—ways in which gray zone strategies reflect something well short of a magic wand of geopolitical advantage.

The most obvious limitation is suggested by the preceding hypothesis. Gray zone strategies allow states to capitalize on others' vulnerabilities, but they seldom, if ever, offer avenues to achieve decisive results on their own. Beijing cannot be certain of achieving its ultimate goals in the South China Sea through gradual gray zone tactics and techniques alone. If others resist sufficiently, China will ultimately need to decide whether to escalate to more elaborate forms of aggression.

For all the recent analysis of gray zone conflicts, for example, there is little evidence that such activities can have conclusive results on their own. Neither the U.S. nor Soviet Cold War-era gray zone efforts appear to have been decisive. (Certainly, the Soviet active measures campaign achieved little of note.) It remains unclear how much China will achieve with its campaign in the South China Sea. Russia's successful grab of Crimea may count as more of a quasi-military *fait accompli* rather than a true gray zone campaign. In short, further research is needed to understand the experience of gray zone strategies.

Just as the defenders in gray zone campaigns face certain dilemmas, so do the aggressors. The more aggressive they are, the more forceful the instruments they employ, the more likely they are to achieve the coercive leverage needed to achieve their objectives. But the higher the degree of force involved, the more likely the gray zone strategist is to provoke a more elaborate response. Galeotti has emphasized the ways in which Russia's campaigns in Ukraine have shown both the potential for and limits of gray zone strategies. The major price paid by Russia due to its operations in Ukraine shows that "this is by no means the guaranteed war-winner some had initially assumed."

Ukraine's resistance hardened, the West imposed severe sanctions, and the campaign went from the intended goal of a short, quick win to a "bleeding wound"[14] that is sapping Russian strength.

In sum, gray zone strategies are not magic wands. They have significant limitations and will be challenging to employ effectively. Their advantage over major warfare is also the source of their weakness: They do not represent strategies capable of achieving decisive outcomes within a defined period of time. States may find great challenges in attempting to achieve defined political objectives reliably with such approaches.

CONCLUSION

These seven hypotheses offer ways of understanding aspects of this emerging form of conflict, perhaps the default means by which measured revisionists (and others) will pursue their political goals in ways more aggressive than classic diplomacy. While the true role of gray zone strategies in world politics remains to be seen, there is at least the potential for it to play a central role in state rivalry in the coming decades, despite its distinct limitations. What remains is to discuss ways in which the United States and its friends and allies can deal with this potential technique, and even use it to their relative advantage.

ENDNOTES - CHAPTER 7

1. Carl von Clausewitz, *On War*, Michael Howard and Peter Paret, eds and trans., Princeton, NJ: Princeton University Press, 1984, p. 593.

2. Amy Chang, Ben FitzGerald, and Van Jackson, "Shades of Gray: Technology, Strategic Competition, and Stability in Maritime Asia," Washington, DC: Center for New American Security, March 2015, pp. 9-10.

3. Thomas Schelling, *The Strategy of Conflict*, New Haven, CT: Yale University Press, 1960, p. 40. See also pp. 4-7, 21-52.

4. Thomas Schelling, *Arms and Influence*, New Haven, CT: Yale University Press, 1966, pp. 97, 105.

5. *Ibid.*, p. 124.

6. Haddick, "America Has No Answer," *War on the Rocks*, February 2014.

7. Andrew Kydd, "Sheep in Sheep's Clothing: Why Security Seekers Do Not Fight Each Other," *Security Studies*, Vol. 7, No. 1, Fall 1997), pp. 116, 125-126. See also Brian C. Rathbun, "Uncertain about Uncertainty: Understanding the Multiple Meanings of a Crucial Concept in International Relations Theory," *International Studies Quarterly*, Vol. 51, 2007. For a pessimistic argument about the potential to resolve uncertainty and avoid security dilemmas, see Sebastian Rosato, "The Inscrutable Intentions of Great Powers," *International Security*, Vol. 39, No. 3, Winter 2014/2015.

8. Robert Powell, "Uncertainty, Shifting Power, and Appeasement," *American Political Science Review*, Vol. 90, No. 4, December 1996, p. 750.

9. "Aware of their weaknesses against the United States and its allies and cognizant of the incalculability of engaging in direct confrontation with the world's most powerful nation," two scholars have argued, a number of key rivals and competitors "engaged instead in a cautious game of 'salami-slicing.' Their strategy is to break deterrence bit by bit, through repeated demonstrations of its insolvency in small, hard-to-counter crises." See A. Wes Mitchel and Jakub Grygiel, "'Salami-Slicing' and Deterrence," *The American Interest*, November 18, 2014.

10. *Ibid.*

11. Schelling, *Arms and Influence*, p. 56.

12. Mark Galeotti, "'Hybrid War' and 'Little Green Men': How It Works and How It Doesn't," E-IR, April 16, 2015, pp. 4-5.

13. Phil Karber, "'Lessons Learned' from the Russo-Ukrainian War," The Russian Military Forum, Washington, DC: Center for Strategic and International Studies, March 10, 2015.

14. Galeotti, pp. 3-4.

CHAPTER 8

STRATEGIES FOR DEALING WITH GRADUALIST CHALLENGES

Responding to gray zone strategies is inherently challenging for the United States, and indeed for any democracy. Competing successfully in this arena demands commitment to steady, coherent, long-term strategies. In some cases, as in responding to clandestine proxy wars, it can require operating in the shadows and taking actions that cannot be publicly acknowledged. It demands an effort to manage narratives in a manner that pushes up against the constraints of democratic policymaking. The United States managed to achieve all of these goals during the Cold War, but, in general, they do not accord well with the typically short-term, absolutist cast of U.S. national security planning.

This is not to suggest that the United States has no tools in its arsenal for such conflicts. In fact, it ought to be able to defend itself and its allies from gray zone aggression perfectly well. Doing so demands integrated strategies that span multiple administrations, but this has been possible in the past. The needed investments are modest, especially because, as Chapter 7 suggested, gray zone strategies are somewhat self-limiting. I will suggest a number of specific capabilities that could be helpful in the tactical back-and-forth of gray zone conflict.

An overarching priority of these steps is to provide senior leaders in the U.S. National Command Authority with a wider range of nuanced options. When confronting gray zone campaigns today, U.S. leaders often confront a typical array of tools not necessarily optimized for gray zone contexts—and not always flexible or tailored to such circumstances. A main priority of any new approach should be to integrate a broad array of potential actions, from long-term work on institutions to immediate responses on the local battlefield, into coherent operational concepts for fighting in the gray zone. U.S. leaders should have a deep and extensive menu of response options for such situations.

RECOMMENDATIONS

Yet, the most fundamental response to this challenge is not to become tactically brilliant in the gray zone—it is to render the zone mostly moot, and take advantage of the inherent limitations and dilemmas involved in the employment of such strategies. These recommendations focus on geopolitical rather than military operational elements. They point to ways of shaping long-term trends in order to render the United States less vulnerable to gray zone disruption.

1. Set the Long-Term Trajectory: Make Sure Time is On Your Side. The fundamental response to gray zone strategies is not to combat them directly, but rather to set the conditions so that long-term social, political, and economic trends favor the United States, its allies and friends, and the stability of the rules-based order. Gray zone strategies prey upon weaknesses and vulnerabilities in these areas. Addressing such potential danger zones is the first step toward becoming more resilient.

The U.S. grand strategy has been built—at least since 1945, in some sense from the very founding of the nation—on the central concept that time was on the side of the American experiment. The central American narrative, and foundation of U.S. grand strategy, is that liberal democracy is destined to triumph over competing ideologies. It was this essential faith that sustained U.S. administrations and generations during the Cold War, and it remains the basic answer to the gray zone campaigns of revisionists today.

The United States could pursue this goal in two broad and complementary ways. One would focus on international and external trends and institutions; one on domestic and internal issues. Internationally, the United States could work to reinforce elements of the rules-based international order that has helped to keep the peace for over 60 years. This approach must evolve, however, to multilateralize the governance of these institutions in important new ways, to open the running of the rules-based order to any responsible state. The United States can use a flexible set of norms and institutions to absorb and normalize the more constrained measured revisionism of rising states like Brazil, Turkey, and India.

Providing democratic, peaceful, and constructive quasi-revisionists with a stake in the system is critical to preserving the overall balance of order and preventing more aggressive revisionists like China and Russia with the opportunity to gather fellow-travelers to some alternative vision of the future system. This does not imply recruiting some of these states as "allies"; none of them has any interest in such a designation. It merely means creating a more shared sense of international ownership of rules, norms, and institutions so that long-term trends can reflect deepened order and strengthened consensus against belligerence. It is a strategy of endorsing partial revisionism to discredit more radical varieties.

Such an approach would build on the idea that, despite their seeming energy and momentum, measured revisionists are operating from a position of weakness. Their bellicosity is ultimately self-defeating—as much so with gray zone aggression as anything else. China's campaign of territorial aggrandizement in the South China Sea has provoked a fairly significant regional response, for example, given that no shots have been fired. Japan's new defense guidance alone and the tighter partnership it implies with the United States has probably cost China more in the overall balance of power than it has gained with its rhetoric and land reclamation. U.S. relations with Japan, Vietnam, the Philippines, and other victims of China's over-reaching have been growing.[1] Russia's even more belligerent gray zone aggression in Ukraine has generated economic sanctions and geopolitical isolation. Truly disruptive revisionism is a dead-end road, and U.S. efforts to manage the future of the rules-based order can build on these natural dynamics and reinforce this lesson. The goal of a strengthened, multilateralized emphasis on norms and institutions is, in part, to create processes and norms that such generate negative feedback.

The second approach to making time work for the United States is the oft-repeated requirement to attend to issues of domestic social and economic strength, from entitlement and tax reform to measures to ease inequality to infrastructure investments and much more. Beyond the United States, socio-economic tension and instability is a key sign of potential vulnerability to gray zone tactics. Russia has been able to gain a foothold in neighboring countries with restive Russian-speaking populations; unhappy, quasi-independent provinces; and weak or corrupt local or central governments.[2] Helping Russia's neighbors to become more stable and well-governed should be a major U.S. focus in responding to gray zone tactics.

Finally, the success of U.S. responses to gray zone aggression will depend in significant measure on whether they are integrated into coherent regional strategies. U.S. success in countering China's South China Sea gray zone approaches will be a function of the degree to which it has an effective larger approach to deal with the growth of Chinese power and foster regional stability. Washington could develop potent capabilities to counter the tactical effects of gray zone campaigns and still fail if its general strategy is ineffectual. This is another example of the multiple ways in which gray zone campaigns must be seen as one piece of a more comprehensive picture: Setting the largest context will be as important to dealing with these challenges as any direct response.

2. **Strengthen Institutions and Norms to Control Revisionist Tactics**. A related but independent response to gray zone aggression is to build or enhance specific norms or institutions designed to reduce the impact or escalatory potential of gray zone tools and techniques.

One example of such norm- and institution-building would be to develop and expand confidence-building and crisis resolution mechanisms, such as processes to enhance transparency at the regional or issue level.[3] One analyst has suggested an expansion of military-to-military contacts, expanded mechanisms for information sharing among partner fleets and militaries, and a more formal system for sharing real-time maritime intelligence.[4]

Beyond transparency and awareness, the United States could work with allies to build codified norms and rules that constrain gray zone adventurism and improve predictability. So far, China has been reluctant to move past informal promises to resolve conflicts peacefully to more elaborate and formalized rules for dispute resolution. The United States could sponsor a new round of dialogues on such initiatives. Globally, it could pursue such ideas as a convention for "cyber rules of the road" that would have the effect of limiting the use of cyber aggression as part of any gray zone campaign. In the process, the United States can build on its status as "partner of choice" to help convene various institutional responses to potential gray zone instability.[5]

Such ideas would also seem tailor-made for parallel Track 2 initiatives, privately funded and engaging researchers in all the regional countries to create a shared historical database and real-time picture of incremental moves throughout the region. These initiatives could take advantage of a number of areas of advancing technology, from grassroots social media reporting to track events to publicly-available civilian imagery.

A particular form of confidence-building mechanism is intensely human, and will be essential in a period of constant rivalry and gray zone conflict: Nurturing leader-to-leader relationships. Nadia Schadlow has emphasized the importance of basic relationship management in the effort to deal with gray zone conflict.[6] Being able to pick up the phone and call a counterpart during a crisis is an essential element of dispute resolution, and yet the practice of building strong personal relationships among senior officials has somewhat fallen out of favor. It will be increasingly important in the fluid, unpredictable world of gray zone campaigns.

3. **Decide Where Accommodation Is Possible**. Not every tool for responding to gray zone aggression must be confrontational. Measured revisionists ultimately desire recognition and stable prosperity. They do not intend to undermine the international system as a whole, and do not, at this point, nourish the hope of sending tank divisions or fleets to seize neighboring territories. It ought to be possible to avoid escalating rounds of gray zone conflict through accommodation.

Accommodation has a negative connotation today, as it is too often equated with appeasement. But great powers must accommodate their mutual interests all the time, and this is no less true — and arguably even more so — at a time of mounting rivalry. Not all gradual efforts to gain influence by other powers must be resisted, and there may be a worthwhile larger dialogue about concessions or negotiations in the name of collective security. The idea is in part to use a measured revisionist's willingness to work gradually to side-step risks of conflict in the short term, while granting some of their goals.

A good example of the soft-line foundation for responding to gray zone pressure may be Vietnam's response to China. It is grounded in a confidence that the two countries share many interests and, despite their occasional conflicts, that Vietnam ought to be able to work its substantial contacts in the Chinese Communist Party in order to resolve key disputes.[7] But it also seems based on a willingness to grant fundamental Chinese interests and not view the competition as a zero-sum game. Accommodation becomes more feasible if, as suggested earlier, the United States has confidence that, due to a combination of strategic realities and U.S. policy, time is on the side of the United States. Such a thought process again goes back to the Cold War, and George Kennan's view—as indeed it was, in different ways, Richard Nixon's and Ronald Reagan's—that when long-term trends were working in America's favor, compromise made sense in the name of keeping the peace.[8]

A good example can be found in Europe today. Few could make the case that long-term trends are favoring Russian power vis-à-vis Europe or the United States. Russia's economy is troubled, it faces a demographic collapse and confronts long-term ecological issues. Now Moscow has incurred a serious economic price in the form of the sanctions imposed in retaliation for its aggression in Ukraine. The United States and its European partners should operate from the view that the long-term will be favorable to their interests relative to Russia's—and that this opens the way to accommodations to prevent escalation of conflict in the short-term. Granting Russia certain concessions regarding its self-defined regional security imperatives could make it less reliant on gray zone campaigns without threatening long-term Western goals.

4. **Build Forces, Systems, Technologies, Concepts, and Doctrines for a Gradualist Environment**. In addition to these broad geostrategic context-setting actions, the United States should also seek to develop specific capabilities optimized for gray zone conflict.

There is evidence that the most effective gray zone campaigns are holistic, integrated approaches that knit together the effects of many different instruments of power. Improving U.S. capabilities for such campaigns thus requires investments in and attention to a wide range of tools and techniques.

To begin with, the United States should build concepts of operations for gray zone conflicts, broad theories of success and planned approaches for employing a range of tools for combined effect. Gray zone campaigns are complex, integrated endeavors, and stumbling into one without a clear sense of how one intends to employ available tools is a prescription for failure. The biggest challenge may be institutional: Deciding what office should develop these concepts. The dilemma is that the military has the most experience with such concept development, but gray zone campaigns are dominantly nonmilitary in nature. Perhaps this calls for a small new office, housed in the State Department or National Security Council, including detailed military officers, civilian experts in other instruments of power, and scholars in the application of coercive diplomacy.

As a general rule, investments in gray zone capabilities ought to cover a wide range of tools. Dominance in any one area is likely to be less important than baseline capabilities in many mutually supporting ones. In general, high-end scenarios suggest the need for quality at the expense of quantity: relatively few high-tech systems that can provide dominant battlefield capabilities. Gray zone conflict typically calls for a wide range of tools.[9]

In terms of specific categories of investment, the descriptions discussed earlier give a good sense of the sorts of areas in which the United States ought to invest. In the information realm, the United States will want improved versions of its current, largely experimental projects to use social media, official content, and other streams of information to shape evolving narratives. In the economic realm, U.S. strategists could perhaps benefit from a more explicit and intensively designed set of options from financial sanctions to anti-corruption strategies to targeted economic assistance. At the higher end of the spectrum, it will want relatively small but dedicated social operations and covert action units uniquely trained for gray zone contexts, likely including regionally-aligned special operations forces with world-class language skills and local socio-political awareness. For maritime environments, the United States will want a better balance between its military and nonmilitary capabilities—suggesting a greater relative investment in the Coast Guard and in medical and humanitarian capabilities. This is only a suggestive list.

As important as any collection of specific capabilities, however, will be a structure and process designed to meld them together into holistic campaigns—and to do so over very long periods of time. It will not be enough to trust that the interagency system will generate effective strategies. Especially because of the multidisciplinary nature of gray zone campaigns, that outcome is unlikely. As problematic as it is to propose yet another structural fix, it may be necessary to create a special office—perhaps at the National Security Council staff, or perhaps within the State Department—to manage the conduct of such campaigns and draw together these various instruments in productive ways and over the long term.

5. **Punish Selected Revisionist Acts and Broadcast True Red Lines**. Finally, research on dealing with incremental efforts to undermine established orders, strategies such as *faits accompli*, suggests the importance of two related responses: Pointed action to punish overly aggressive revisionism, and broadcasting clear red lines for truly vital interests.

In service of the first goal, noticeable punishments must be imposed on an aggressor who flouts international norms with their gray zone revisionism. The United States and its allies can build cost-imposing strategies to render gray zone campaigns toxic drains on resources and reputation. One example might be a covert campaign to strengthen Ukrainian militias fighting Russian proxies. "By turning what Moscow had hoped would be a quick limited war into a prolonged war of attrition," two scholars suggest, "it would be clear that revising the existing order by force is not cost-effective. The salami slicing, so to speak, would be halted and the hand holding the knife rapped across the knuckles."[10]

The basic concept behind such approaches would be to build engines of negative feedback for aggressive revisionist acts, which create cost-imposing dynamics that make these self-limiting and declining techniques. As Thomas Schelling has argued:

> When the act to be deterred is inherently a sequence of steps whose cumulative effect is what matters, a threat geared to the increments may be more credible than one that must be carried out either all at once or not at all when some particular point has been reached. It may even be impossible to define a 'critical point' with sufficient clarity to be persuasive.[11]

Put in the plain language for which Schelling is justly revered, the essay continues: "The man who would kick a dog should be threatened with modest punishment for each step toward the dog, even though his proximity is of no interest in itself."[12] U.S. strategists need to develop a similar expectation of action-reaction dynamics for gray zone conflicts, to make clear to potential aggressors that they will pay a specific price for each of their incremental steps—and that there are red lines which will trigger much more substantial escalation.

In this context, Schelling argues for a sort of muscular gradualism. A threat, to be made more credible, "can be decomposed into a series of consecutive smaller threats," giving the deterring state "an opportunity to demonstrate on the first few transgressions that the threat will be carried out on the rest."[13] He gives the example of a desire to get reforms on an aid recipient's policies. Cancelling all aid may be too difficult, and counterproductive. So an aid donor might make a series of small threats, to cancel individual programs or grants, and in fulfilling them build leverage to get its larger wishes granted.

This is the crux of the challenge, however—the political price for punishing these small steps seems very high to many U.S. friends and allies. This is a dilemma measured revisionism creates. However, the fact is that the more the revisionists push, the stronger the balancing becomes—a trend we see today in Europe and Asia with the reactions to Russian and Chinese revisionist muscle-flexing.[14] U.S. policy can build on this dynamic to create even more potent examples of coercive reactions to gray zone aggression.

An important requirement for such approaches is to look for and use moments when the gray zone aggressor overreaches. A central component of gray zone responses is to build up a gradual contrary portrait of the author of the campaign as an irresponsible and dangerous violator of international norms. When a gray zone campaign generates unplanned tension— as when a maritime clash results in fatalities, or a low-level commander goes too far, or paramilitary operations intended to remain secret are unveiled—the

United States can use the momentary anger to achieve specific objectives in its own countergray zone campaign. It can align coalitions against the aggressors, try to put formalized rules of the road on the books, pull targeted states away from aggressors' economic inducements, and more. The idea is, over time, to use excessive steps to place a spotlight on the overall campaigns so as to complicate the efforts of the gray zone strategists to achieve long-term progress.

In the process, a second critical requirement is to make true red lines clear — and enforce them. Daniel Altman has argued in relation to *faits accompli* that:

> More often than not, the best option available to a state confronting this problem is to rely on a strong red line set on a focal point to encapsulate many small units of value that this state cannot credibly threaten to defend individually. Knowing it cannot mount a credible defense after abandoning this red line, that point becomes one from which it cannot retreat without greater cost.[15]

He argues that Cold War tensions eased when the two sides developed a partly de facto set of clear red lines (in places like the inter-Korean border) that rules out a continual series of *faits accomplis*.

This range of alternatives could offer a basic framework for dealing with gray zone revisionism. The most important requirement, however, is to understand and take seriously gray zone conflict as a distinct category of state action. This monograph represents a first step toward a more comprehensive understanding of gray zone conflict. As noted at the outset, it is far from the last word. Its goal is to provoke more discussion and thinking about a strategic challenge that is likely to continue confronting the United States and its friends and allies in the years ahead.

ENDNOTES - CHAPTER 8

1. Keith Johnson, "Pushing Back Against a Chinese Lake in the South China Sea," *Foreign Policy*, April 28, 2015.

2. This issue is highlighted as a critical condition of successful gray zone approaches in András Ràcz, Russia's Hybrid War in Ukraine, Helsinki, Finland: The Finnish Institute of International Affairs, June 2015, pp. 76-81.

3. Van Jackson has argued that "Gray zone coercion loses much of its efficacy in an environment rendered transparent. If a would-be aggressor knows it will be seen as such by its neighbors, that transparency may have the effect of deterring gray zone coercion." Van Jackson, Testimony before the House Committee on Foreign Affairs, Subcommittee on Asia and the Pacific, Washington, DC, February 26, 2015, p. 6. He suggests two initiatives to achieve this goal: Boosting regional military-to-military ties, and cooperative efforts to enhance maritime surveillance and awareness. "Information sharing regimes intended to increase operational transparency exist as a patchwork at the bilateral and trilateral level in Asia," Jackson points out, suggesting that "greater situational awareness—ideally in real time—would benefit the region as a whole and increase the political costs of gray zone coercion or other forms of military adventurism.

4. Robert Haddick, "Six Ways to Respond to China's Salami-Slicing Tactics," *The National Interest*, November 24, 2014.

5. The "convening function" argument is made in Boston Global Forum, "Recent Trends in the South China Sea Disputes," June 2015, p. 11.

6. Nadia Schadlow, "Peace and War: The Space Between," *War on the Rocks*, August 2014.

7. Christopher Yung and Patrick McNulty, "China's Tailored Coercion," Report 5, Maritime Strategy Series, Washington, DC: Center for a New American Security, January 26, 2015.

8. George F. Kennan, "Measures Short of War," The George F. Kennan Lectures at the National War College, 1946-1947, Washington, DC: National Defense University Press, 1991.

9. Zachary Keck, "Is Air-Sea Battle Useless?" *The National Interest*, May 16, 2014.

10. A. Wess Mitchell and Jakob Grygiel, "'Salami-Slicing' and Deterrence," *The American Interest*, November 18, 2014. They also recommend much more powerful actions—which they describe as "proportional." In this case, they suggest "working to foment internal problems in Russia's more troublesome regions." But they recognize that NATO lacks the willpower to take such bold action. In any event, I would consider such acts to be far too provocative.

11. Thomas Schelling, *The Strategy of Conflict*, New Haven, CT: Yale University Press, 1960, p. 42.

12. *Ibid.*

13. *Ibid.*, p. 41.

14. Jonathan Holslag, "The Smart Revisionist," *Survival*, Vol. 56, No. 5, October-November 2014, pp. 110-111. Joshua Rivner argues that the West should essentially do nothing in response to Putin's gray zone aggressions, because the outcomes have been so unambiguously bad for Russia that the actions are weakening rather that strengthening Russian power; see Joshua Rovner, "Dealing with Putin's Strategic Incompetence," *War on the Rocks*, August 12, 2015.

15. Daniel Altman, "Red Lines and Faits Accomplis," Ph.D. dissertation, Cambridge, MA: Massachusetts Institute of Technology, 2015, p. 26. He also makes the point that proportional responses may not be enough, p. 27.

U.S. ARMY WAR COLLEGE

Major General William E. Rapp
Commandant

*****

STRATEGIC STUDIES INSTITUTE
and
U.S. ARMY WAR COLLEGE PRESS

Director
Professor Douglas C. Lovelace, Jr.

Director of Research
Dr. Steven K. Metz

Author
Dr. Michael J. Mazarr

Editor for Production
Dr. James G. Pierce

Publications Assistant
Ms. Rita A. Rummel

*****

Composition
Mrs. Jennifer E. Nevil

Made in the USA
San Bernardino, CA
02 October 2017